'A book full of authentic faith a
Bottle is the sort of encourageme
whole of ourselves to the One w]

Revd David K. Mayne, lead p......,
Shoeburyness & Thorpe Bay Baptist Church,
Moderator, Baptist Union Council

'Once again Jeannie Kendall heads straight for the emotions
many prefer to leave unexamined, as she guides the reader
through to understand something of the complexity of tears in
different situations, and the relevance and depth of the Bible
for contemporary life. This book is unsettling in a most con-
structive way.'

Dr Rachel Johnson, former research librarian, University of
Worcester, currently working at Tyndale House, Cambridge

'In this her second book, Jeannie has produced something
that is both compelling and yet challenging, delightful and yet
distressing. The raw reality of the modern situations she has
selected are interwoven with her depictions of the stories of
biblical characters. Her added thoughts and reflections com-
plement both her amazing storytelling and insightful research.
I fully endorse and recommend it, since it will help the reader
with the tears of their own journey.'

David Simmonds, director, S.E. Hampshire Healing Rooms

'In these pages Jeannie offers us distilled wisdom, compassion
and understanding as we navigate the world of our tears and
emotions and come to terms with what it means to be fully
human.'

Paul Tyas, fellow traveller

'Jeannie's exploration of tears is both intimately personal and universally relevant: it is full of engaging stories told with compassion and deep empathy. She writes with an ease of language that facilitates reading though the content is far from simple. The text effortlessly weaves together real-life human responses to challenging circumstances with theological reflection and psychological education. Having recently read *Held in Your Bottle* I feel more fully human and more fully alive with my own emotional world.'

Ruth Dormandy, psychotherapist, clinical and pastoral supervisor

'Infused with the emotion of personal experiences and set in the context of biblical narrative, this book can assist us in processing our own tearful responses to situations and issues, acknowledging that God is ever present, holding, accepting and shaping us.'

Rosanne Tyas, professional lead for Music Therapy at the Royal Hospital for Neurodisability, Putney, London

'I found Jeannie's first book helpful both for myself and to recommend to others. I think this one is even better. As a man who has been known to cry at adverts (and, yes, football results), the subject of tears is always fascinating. As a minister, I have the privilege of sitting with people as they shed tears for different reasons. As a member of L'Arche London, I have shared tears of joy and sorrow and grief on many occasions. *Held in Your Bottle* movingly captures different stories of different tears and puts them in both a biblical and contemporary context, helping us to make sense of these salty drops. Read it – you'll cry!'

Gerry Stanton, Baptist minister and development director of Wave: We're All Valued Equally

'I can never remember having read a book before that tackles the subject of tears from a Christian perspective. With its blend of contemporary stories, reworked biblical narrative and psychological insights, it draws attention to the variety of meanings that tears have and how they are part of our emotional toolkit. I trust, like Jeannie, that this book will encourage us to value our tears, as the Lord does, and to reflect on what they mean for us.'

Tricia McIlroy, counselling course leader at Spurgeon's College

'This is an important book. Tears speak with an eloquence that words rarely convey, and Jeannie Kendall explores this theme with great sensitivity and power. The contemporary stories that she draws on are exceptionally poignant, and the way in which she explores appropriate Bible passages is imaginative and insightful. Jeannie draws on a wealth of personal experience not only within her own family, but as a counsellor and minister. In my teens I concluded that I could never be a minister because I cried too easily. Happily, I discovered how wrong that was, and I thank God for the blessing of tears throughout my ministry. Jeannie helps us to understand just what a blessing they are.'

Jonathan Edwards, former General Secretary of the
Baptist Union of Great Britain and now adviser
to Through the Roof and other Christian disability charities

'As with her first book, Jeannie skilfully interweaves human stories of tears in a variety of situations with biblical events, followed by insightful reflections. Invaluable both for those experiencing painful situations and those seeking to understand and support. Highly recommended.'

Julie Aylward, prison chaplain

'Jeannie Kendall combines an imaginative re-telling of scriptural stories with a keen psychological and spiritual perspective that enables the reader to enter into the ways in which tears reveal our deepest emotions, and offer these back to God. In the bottle of God's encompassing love, our tears are never forgotten.'

Revd Dr Paul Goodliff, General Secretary, Churches Together in England, Associate Research Fellow and tutor, Spurgeon's College and visiting lecturer in Ecumenism and Christian Doctrine, University of Roehampton

'*Held in Your Bottle* is a book that I believe is possibly a first for the Christian book market. It will inspire, restore, heal and evoke emotions in you that may have never been exposed before. As a person who finds tears hard to come by, this super read has opened my eyes to a whole new world. A book that is so relevant for today and a bestseller in the making.'

Dave Lock, manager, Manna Christian Centre Christian Bookshop; and committee member, Christian Booksellers Group for the Booksellers Association in Great Britain and Ireland

'This is Jeannie's second book and to write it she has searched deep into her own personal experiences, and those of others who have shared their stories. Sensitively written, it is an exploration of the different tears we experience as we go through life, their meaning and perhaps God's purpose in them. This is not a book to be rushed, but one to be savoured and returned to. I was quite moved by some of it, and it gave me a deeper understanding of why I sometimes feel how I do.'

Cedric Pierce, former railwayman and professional in the criminal justice system

'Another excellent book from Jeannie Kendall, written with such honesty and insight. As you read the book there are few chapters you won't be able to identify with, either through the personal or biblical stories told or in the way Jeannie brings them together in a reflection which allows you to know it is OK to cry. The book confirms there are no easy answers but encourages us to understand that God sees, hears and feels our pain, which is a great comfort to know, and allows us to embrace and celebrate our tears rather than hide them away. This book is a great resource for personal use, as well as a great tool for counsellors, ministers and those involved in caring for people in distress.'

Linda Abel Boanerges, director of Practical Training and Admissions, Spurgeon's College

Held in Your Bottle

Exploring the value of tears in the Bible and in our lives today

Jeannie Kendall

Authentic

First published 2021 by Authentic Media Limited,
PO Box 6326, Bletchley, Milton Keynes, MK1 9GG
authenticmedia.co.uk

27 26 25 24 23 22 21   7 6 5 4 3 2 1

British Library Cataloguing in Publication Data
A catalogue record for this book is available from the British Library.
ISBN: 978-1-78893-171-7
978-1-78893-172-4 (e-book)

Cover design by Vivian Hansen
Printed and bound by CPI Group (UK) Ltd, Croydon, CR0 4YY

Contents

To all those friends who have encouraged me that I had another book inside me: especially David Mayne who, as someone once said, 'does friendship well': for his indefatigable support and many exchanges on Messenger.

To those who have held my tears and walked, both literally and metaphorically, with me – you know who you are.

To those who across the years and for this book have been willing to share with me their tears, or their stories of tears.

To my precious family, always held in my heart.

And above all, to the God who holds all my tears in his bottle.

Foreword by Adrian Plass

I met Jeannie some years ago, but most of what I consider a very warm friendship has been conducted via the selectively magical medium of email. I have a great fondness for her, not least because she has been unfailingly supportive, sometimes at times when she cannot have imagined how much her kind words meant to me. I am such a wide-eyed child, unsurprisingly drawn to people who seem to like and approve of me.

Yes, all that is true, but now, as Jeannie would readily understand, being a 'professional Christian' like myself, I am obliged to be honest. She has annoyed me just a little. You see, I happen to be very familiar with the fifty-sixth Psalm. First (regrettably, but not to the point of tears) for flippant reasons. There is a version that renders the first verse as follows:

'Be merciful to me, O God, for men hotly pursue me . . .'[1]

At speaking events thirty years ago, my rather pathetic assertion that this might be the cry of a woman who is wearied by the effect of her looks on the male population was greeted with consternation from (metaphorically) the expensive seats at the front, and ribald laughter from the cheap seats at the back. This has nothing to do with why I am annoyed. I just wanted to enjoy saying it again.

No, it's all about the bit that Jeannie mentions in her Introduction. In the eighth verse David talks about God storing his tears in a bottle. That always fascinated me. I enjoyed playing with the idea that, in some impossible, miraculous sense, God has billions of tear-filled bottles stored on shelves in an inconceivably massive heavenly warehouse. I wanted to write a book about a young angel writing regular letters to someone on earth. One of the things I was really looking forward to was my novice angel's experience of being taken by God to view the divine Bottle Bank for himself. How would he describe the scene in his next letter to earth? How would his correspondent deal with such a dramatic, tear-soaked image?

When my publisher asked me about possibilities for another book, I offered two options. One was the angel story. The other was a novel about someone called The Shadow Doctor, a strange man whose task was to help people to face and deal with the dark places in their lives. He chose the latter. I was not sure about that then, but now I am very glad. I was able to produce two Shadow Doctor books that changed my life in the writing.

The annoying thing is that Jeannie has written a better book on the subject of tears and real people and a real God than I could ever have put together. My overambitious idea had been to use the angel concept to seriously ground the things of God in genuine experience and biblical context and careful, properly informed analysis of the issues that would be covered. Jeannie has succeeded in doing exactly that. Goodness knows how she managed to persuade people to share their lives in such an open and sometimes harrowing way. They must have felt very safe indeed. I suppose I might have had a go at the scriptural connections and parallels, but the third part of each section, the reflection followed by – thank God! – genuinely open questions, takes the reader down into a safe, more uncompromising and vividly challenging landing that I could never have managed to negotiate with such skill and awareness.

So, I forgive you, dear Jeannie, for providing such a timely, and necessarily honest support for all those who know about tears shed for a myriad of reasons. By the way, I too found tears forming in my eyes during the trailer for *Bambi*. I hope that makes you feel a little bit better. God bless you. This book is filled with your heart.

Introduction

There are many comparisons made between writing a book and giving birth. But certainly I did not expect that having literally just seen my first book[1] delivered, I would already be setting out on the 'pregnancy' of the next one. It seems that God had other plans.

Books, like babies, are conceived in many different circumstances, and this one had an interesting start in life. Searching the internet while studying for a sermon, I came across something which intrigued me. A photographer called Rose-Lynn Fisher had published a book of tears – her own and others – cried in different circumstances and viewed under a microscope.[2] The results were fascinating, and beautiful.

Certainly scientists have known for some time that there are three kinds of tears, with slightly different chemical components: basal tears (those which keep our eyes hydrated), reflex tears (in response to an irritation such as grit or peeling onions) and psychic tears (those cried in distress, happiness and so on). Although we cannot be sure, it seems that only humans cry psychic tears. Some species of animals appear to have emotions,[3] yet only have basal and reflex tears.[4] The sheer variety of photographs from the work of Rose-Lynn Fisher made me think about the myriad of tears shed by various characters in the Bible. What might we learn from them about what it means to be fully human, and how might that link with what we know about our emotions from other sources? Curiously, during the week where I had sent the proposal to Authentic but not yet shared that with anyone, in our evening service one of the congregation spoke out in a time of quiet that he had a picture of tears. He went on to interpret the picture in other ways, but the timing was somehow reassuring.

I wanted in addition to relate this biblical exploration to my own tears – which has made this book in many ways intensely personal. I have to confess that for years I had an ambivalent attitude to them. Rightly or wrongly, I received the impression whilst growing up that tears – or indeed any expression of emotion – was not a good idea. I suspect both my parents struggled with their emotions in different ways, and I don't think they intended to give me that message – children often draw inaccurate conclusions as they try with limited experience and emotional vocabulary to make sense of the world. The result, however, was that I became ashamed of my tears. If I was about to cry, for example at a film (I have to this day not seen *Bambi* as I wept at the trailer), I would hide, both to regain control and also so as not to be seen. For some decades, despite fearing public tears, I was also afraid to cry in private because, having bottled them up so efficiently, I feared they would be overwhelming if I was alone with no one to somehow help me stop. At this point in my life, however, I am more, if not entirely, at peace with them. There are times – for example, when conducting the funeral of someone I knew particularly well and cared deeply for – that it is necessary to hold them in check, at least for a time. But at other times I let them flow, and feel no shame. My family lovingly tease me that I cry regularly at films, finding particularly amusing my copious tears at the death of Darth Vader, the evil character in *Star Wars*. Yet I do indeed find that scene almost unbearably poignant, as the inherent humanity and even compassion is revealed behind the mask which has allowed evil to dominate. My tears may at times be mildly inconvenient, but I would not be without them now, even though at times I am not even entirely sure what has brought them about.

Tears can also, I believe, be a gift of the Spirit, and part of catching God's heart of compassion for his world. In prayer, for example, as I explore later in the book, tears can often be an expression of what the apostle Paul – no stranger to tears himself – describes as the Spirit interceding for us with 'wordless groans'.[5] At such times undoubtedly our own sadnesses and losses are part of the mix, as John Goldingay so helpfully points out,[6] but I do not believe that invalidates the experience. It seems to me that one of the wonderful things about the Christian faith is the belief that God both honours and chooses to use our humanity.

It may be that you are in a particular season of tears, whether of grief or joy, or the many other kinds of weeping. In that case you may be drawn to particular chapters. I hope, however, you will in time read them all, whether because that particular season draws towards a close, or from a desire to join me on the wider journey of exploration. We are complex creatures who are 'fearfully and wonderfully made'[7] and I believe that our emotions are as God-created as our bodies and minds. As such they are to be celebrated, not feared or suppressed.

I have been reminded again as I wrote what an extraordinarily relevant and realistic book the Bible is. Within its pages, we find both men and women weeping, and every kind of human emotion in all its raw vulnerability. I have certainly not exhausted in this book all the examples I could have used. I have long believed that Jesus was actually the most fully emotional person who ever lived, his expression of feelings unfettered by some of the things which hold us back. His own tears feature in this book. Tears are our first form of communication when we are born and an integral part of our humanity.

The title of the book comes from Psalm 56:8, which in the *New Living Translation* reads:

> You keep track of all my sorrows.
> You have collected all my tears in your bottle.
> You have recorded each one in your book.

This psalm – part of the Hebrew worship book – is attributed to King David, a character who experienced several extreme circumstances and the attendant emotions, and who we will come back to later. I have often quoted these words to people, especially when they were unsure if their emotion was acceptable to God. The reply is often: 'He must have a very big bottle.' I believe he has – enough to capture all their and my tears, give them dignity, and somehow hold them as he holds each of us.

Each chapter has the same format. Firstly, there is a story from today, of someone's tears cried for reasons linked with the topic of the chapter, written in the first person. Some are my own stories, and some are from others, of both genders, who were willing to share them and for which I am very grateful. Then I have retold the story of the tears of a Bible character shed in a context linked with the topic explored in that chapter, seeking to identify either with them or with someone who was part of their story. I would encourage you to read the whole of the Bible passages that are cited for each chapter. You can

Google them if you don't have a Bible and it will help what I say about the stories make a lot more sense. *The Message* version is good for reading the stories in a fresh way.

The third section reflects on both the passage and the theme, drawing on insights from various sources and my previous trainings in teaching, counselling and theology in an accessible way. Some chapters are longer than others because the issues they raise are more complex, but I wanted to capture the range of tears that we experience and which the Bible accounts reflect.

This book can be read individually, or in a small group setting as a way both to study the Bible but also to facilitate sharing honestly together. There are some questions at the end of each chapter to try to help your reflection. They are just a starting point: don't let them confine you. In whatever context you read it, I hope that this book will not only help you to look at the Bible in a fresh way, but also assist you in more fully accepting and understanding both your own emotional life and that of others, and to know that God treasures it all.

It has been my great privilege, particularly in my years as a counsellor and then as a minister, to witness the tears of many people in a host of different situations. Each precious encounter has been an important part of making me who I am today, and so helped both me and this book to grow. Thank you, all.

I completed the writing of this book during a time of many tears as the Covid-19 pandemic raged across the world, claiming many lives and bringing untold distress in so many ways. I do not know what the situation will be by the time you read this, but it was a reminder to me of the importance of holding on to the fact that our tears are held by God, as we are, even amidst the most difficult of times.

Part One

Different Tears

1

Tears of Regret

Esau . . . for a single meal sold his inheritance rights as the oldest son. Afterwards, as you know, when he wanted to inherit this blessing, he was rejected. Even though he sought the blessing with tears, he could not change what he had done.[1]

So, with my thanks to our first brave contributor, we begin our journey.

A current story of tears of regret

I have always found regret hard to acknowledge. I tended to think that the circumstances that caused me pain had been caused by things that were out of my control and so felt I had nothing to regret. I have not always looked at the part I may have played and what I could have done differently to prevent the difficulties. Regret, in my opinion, had always seemed pointless and not a good use of my time or energy, believing it was too late to feel it when I could not change anything. I preferred to move on quickly. I felt that to regret would be just another burden, that it would only produce in me a constant nagging sense of guilt. To cry over the things I regretted seemed to me to be showing weakness, and I thought that my tears would be wasted and pointless.

I knew in theory that God has given us tears for a reason, but having been brought up in house where tears were frowned upon, the tendency was always to push them aside and ignore them. I grew up with a father who, due to the nature of his generation and the job he did, taught me to be stoical and to try to keep my feelings hidden.

However, I finally reached a point in my life where I was confronted with feelings of regret over and over again, and they would not go away. Moving into a flat on my own after a long marriage, bringing up a family and then a lengthy divorce, brought to my door unwelcome opportunities to acknowledge my feelings. Unexpectedly, the emotions intruded and would not go away. I was forced to reconcile with them and to finally feel the regret I had avoided. Living in a new area where there was no background noise from my children (now grown and moved on), animals and other familiar neighbourhood sounds, memories of the past came flooding back like a music track stuck on a loop, forcing me to shed tears which I could not always understand. They were unwelcome, and I would try to push them away, and go out to escape them. However, the tears would follow me everywhere – to the park, to church, to work, even in front of a cheerful film, randomly coming and going in an infuriating way.

So, what were these regrets? I regretted drinking too much and causing my marriage to get off to a rocky start through my foolish behaviour. I regretted not taking more care and responsibility for my drinking habits sooner and not seeking God earlier for answers to my alcoholism. I had let things slide for too long, and in the long run it made things more difficult to repair in my marriage. I also regretted the impact it had on my children and the bad example I had set them.

When I married, I had no idea I was an alcoholic and therefore had little understanding of my addictive behaviour and the consequences it had for other people, particularly my husband and children. Instead, I blamed everything on other factors in my life, such as a bereavement early in my childhood. More recently, since recognising my alcoholism and attending therapy groups, I have come to realise that we need to face and accept our hurt and fear, take responsibility, ask for forgiveness where we have hurt others, forgive ourselves and seek to move forward. At times this all seems too difficult and I would prefer not to dwell too deeply on it all. I can have compassion for others but struggle to feel it for myself. I prefer to conceal and preserve my vulnerabilities both from myself and others. However, I have learned through the compassion of God and his people that tears can be healing and can also be a part of expressing repentance and both giving and receiving forgiveness.

The AA 12-step programme teaches alcoholics to seek forgiveness and own and admit to behaviours that have caused harm to people. Since joining AA eight years ago, the meetings, as well as meditation, prayer and taking communion at church, have given me opportunities to repent, ask for forgiveness and to release the tears to God. These tears have brought healing and warmth into my life and a steady but slow progression towards freedom from the past.

Unless we face regret head-on, I believe it will only fester. Sometimes I have found that circumstances have thrown up opportunities to again express my regret, and given me permission to cry and ask God for help. At times we can be reminded of our mistakes and failures, past and present, but each time this happens I have found that shedding tears in safe places has brought me more of an understanding of myself, my story and the loving and compassionate way that God really sees me.

For me, feeling and acknowledging regret was, among other things, about taking responsibility for my actions. Freedom for personal growth continues to come as I learn to forgive myself. Acknowledging regret, I have learned to love myself as God loves me, and yes, that includes letting the tears flow without shame.

Reflecting on the Bible account: Esau's story

It's all over. Everything. The whole journey of my life that was leading to this moment is now reduced to nothing, like ravaging locusts leaving ragged stalks as a reminder of what has been lost. I'm nothing, nobody, and all I have are the tears rolling down my cheeks and the bitter taste of regret for what might have been.

Ever since I was old enough to be fully aware of him, I recognised that my brother envied me, and that our family was split down the middle: my father favouring me as the eldest and my mother preferring Jacob as if to compensate. It was all unspoken, but the divided favouritism hung in the air of our tent like smoke after a fire, and at times it seemed to choke my soul.

But I told myself it did not matter, because I was the eldest, the one who brought my father his favourite meats. So, in the end I would prevail, I would come out on top. My brother could grasp all he wanted, but I would push him away just as, according to our mother's tale, I had done at our birth. No one and nothing could stop me, and in my arrogance, it never occurred to me that I was riding for a fall.

You will judge me for my story, I suppose – but perhaps it is all too easy to sneer from a lofty moral hill. Have you never been taken over by your appetite, of any kind? Felt overcome by a force you could not resist, been too impatient to think through the consequences of your actions, as I was that day?

I was ravenous. Hunting is skilful but physically demanding, and it takes it out of a man. Jacob with his homely life never recognised that, but I guess none of us ever really understand each other, and I suppose that we never fully see the truth about ourselves, either. So that day I got home to find him cooking my favourite stew, standing over the fire, stirring quietly, while every bone and muscle I possessed was aching with fatigue and my stomach was growling like a wild beast.

All I wanted was that food. I could think of nothing else, and to begin with I thought he was joking when he asked for my birthright, my place at the table as eldest, in exchange. I laughed, but then stopped as I caught the glint in his eye and realised he was serious. I should have hesitated, should have thought just for a moment, but as the red mist of my desire descended, I swapped my future for a moment's pleasure. As I swore the oath I almost wavered, but with my eyes drawn to the cooking pot I carried on like an animal swept away in a swollen river.

So, I ate the meal, and of course it was soon forgotten, and with it all my foolishness.

Until another momentous day. My father's eyes were growing dim with the ravages of age, his youth just a faded memory. He thought about death often, as if his failing sight reminded him that his life was in a twilight time too. So, he called me to hunt for him, to bring him his favourite food, his capacity to taste as good as ever and his one remaining pleasure.

I could curse my brother as I remember. And my mother too, were it not that I owe her my life. She overheard my father's request, and between them they plotted to rob me of my father's blessing, his last bequest to me. She cooked a meal to my father's favourite recipe and covered Jacob's arms with skin to feel like mine. So, while I blithely hunted in the forest, secure in what was to come, it was being stolen from me. The precious, affirming words which should have been mine went to him, and could not be taken back. The scheming, selfish villain I can hardly bear to call my brother had taken what was mine. Where was God in all that?

It is not fair, and I don't think I will ever forgive him. Or, perhaps, myself. And again, memory fresh in the recalling, I weep.

(This part of Esau's story is found in Genesis 25:19–34 and Genesis 27.)

I think that there are very few of us who could say with honesty that there is nothing that we regret. Most of us have those moments when we wake in the night and replay something that we wish we could rewind – from a trivial and foolish unguarded word through to a catastrophic decision with far-reaching consequences. Regret is arguably a universal human emotion – it used to be thought that only those with antisocial personality disorder (sometimes referred to as sociopaths or psychopaths) did not experience regret, but now even that has been questioned.[2]

Whilst writing this chapter I asked several groups of people what they or others regretted most. The answers were very varied, but with some common themes:

- Missed opportunities, including from fear;
- Missing an opportunity to say something positive and encouraging;
- Not reconciling with, or visiting, before someone died;
- More generally falling out with people or saying things in anger which could not be unsaid;
- Not speaking up or being direct with others, including about feelings;
- Not going with a first instinct, and bad decisions generally;
- Worrying too much about what others thought, or living up to their expectations;
- Taking physical or mental health for granted and not looking after them enough;
- Wasted time, in particular being too busy to be with the people that really matter.

These examples are indicative of the different types of regret we experience. The first kind is regret for decisions we ourselves have made, or actions we have taken. The story where Esau chooses to sell his birthright for a meal is one of these, putting immediate gratification ahead of consideration of the long-term consequences. This is something many of us are familiar with – if only when that delicious pudding sabotages our weigh-in that week. There are two varieties of regret over our own actions. The first is regret we experience because in retrospect we realise how something could have been different had we possessed information or wisdom we have now – genuine mistakes. The second is regret where we knew what we know now but went ahead anyway – actions based entirely on our own foolishness or waywardness.

I suspect, and some psychologists agree,[3] that in the short term we most regret things that we *have* done, because the memory, and perhaps the sense of shame, are fresh and raw. However, if our regrets concern recent events, we may at least be able to take action. We can try to repair relationships, such as by taking responsibility, apologising and explaining, or change things in some way, such as moving on from that job we regret taking and so on. In contrast, over the long-term we are more likely to regret the things we have *not* done – such as opportunities we have not taken – as the results of these inactions may only be perceived over time and it is sometimes too late to alter the consequences. We also process our feelings about action and inaction differently because not acting does not usually produce the same intensity of guilt and shame as an action.

Regret, however, is not solely based on things over which we had control. We can also regret things which might have been, where we were not the decision-makers – the job we were not offered, or the relationship which never happened, or floundered, because the other person did not feel the same. We wonder how our lives might have been changed if our circumstances had been different, or others had chosen a particular path which would have impacted us. In the first story in this chapter, for example, might things have been different without the early bereavement and with a different upbringing? We can never know, but can carry a sense of regret nonetheless.

It seems possible that at least in one area, men and women may differ in regard to regret. Generally, research has found no difference between men and women with regard to the kind of things they regret, but the one exception is romantic relationships. One fascinating piece of research found that women regret equally things which were done and not done, whereas men more frequently regretted inaction.[4]

The impact of regret on our wellbeing will depend on various factors. In the best scenario, it can lead us to reassess certain aspects of our lives and so to do things differently in the future – such as the earlier example where the writer, regretting the effects of previous drinking, began and has maintained a life of abstinence. The choices we make at these moments of insight are crucial. Saul, the first king of Israel, had a kingship which went badly wrong. It would seem that when David, who was to become the next king, came on to the scene, Saul saw in him the king that he might have been. Instead of using this to spur him on to better things, he developed a murderous rage, which lead to numerous attempts on David's life. Using regret as a motivation to facilitate change is only possible, of course, where we have some control over what we want to alter in the future. If we cannot, then the risk is that we continue to ruminate – such as in those waking in the night moments or other times where we constantly replay actions or conversations. If this continues, particularly if combined with self-blame, it can clearly have a considerably detrimental effect on us until we can find a way to reconcile with the past. It seems that age and mental health may also be a factor in our ability to do that: generally, healthy older people are less inclined to look back with regret when there is nothing more that can be done, but those who are depressed tend to still hold on to regrets.[5]

Our ability to forgive both others and ourselves is key in offsetting the damaging effects of regret we find difficult to relinquish. Better understanding ourselves and what led us to the action or inaction we regret can help in that process. It is interesting that Esau, who like Saul experienced murderous rage,[6] is later able to reconcile with his brother, Jacob.[7] Genesis follows Jacob's story but not Esau's, so we can only surmise that the years they spent apart, with Jacob in exile, gave Esau the opportunity to rethink the part he had played in the breakdown of their relationship.

One of the most poignant contrasts in the Bible is between Judas and Peter. Judas betrayed Jesus, revealing his whereabouts to the authorities, which led to Jesus' arrest and ultimately his death.[8] There is much speculation about Judas's motive, the most usual being that he wanted to force Jesus' hand to begin a revolution to overthrow the Romans, misunderstanding the nature of Jesus' mission, but ultimately, we cannot know his reasons. Peter, waiting outside Jesus' trial, denied knowing Jesus to a serving girl and two other strangers, resulting in his own bitter tears of regret.[9] Judas, tortured by regret, killed himself.[10] Peter, broken as he clearly was, still chose to remain with the disciples, was met by Jesus after the resurrection,[11] and was later movingly restored as Jesus three times invited him afresh to his pastoral calling, a gentle reworking of the sting of the three denials.[12]

Part of our humanity means that we will inevitably make mistakes and so have regrets. One of the great gospel truths is that because of the death of Jesus for us, we can find forgiveness and a new start. Allowing that to help us forgive ourselves can be challenging, but without doubt, life-transforming.

Some questions to reflect on

- Think of some of the things in your life you have regretted. Have they been things you have done, or things you haven't done?
- Think of a regret you are living with at the moment, if any. Is there something you can learn from it for the future?
- How easy do you find it to accept forgiveness from God or others, and to forgive yourself?
- Is there a regret that you might find it helpful to talk to a trusted friend or counsellor about?

2

Tears of Family Pain

*All his sons and daughters came to comfort him,
but he refused to be comforted. 'No,' he said, 'I
will continue to mourn until I join my son in the
grave.' So his father wept for him.*[1]

A current story of tears of family pain

'Aah!' A big sigh escapes my lips. I feel the pain in my heart
pinning me to the bean bag in the prayer room. Will it ever get
any better, I wonder? My eyes rest on my eldest daughter, sitting at the table painting something on blue paper. She seems
very focused.

It's nearly midnight and we are at our local Baptist church
in the quiet upper room. I have brought my daughter with me
seeking refuge in God's house for the night, because I do not
believe that we would have survived on our own the approaching cyclone which seemed to threaten our sanity. We are bur-
dened by so much pain. My daughter has lost her faith in God
but is hanging onto her trust in me, but I have lost my trust in
my own ability and am now clinging tightly onto my faith in
God. He gifted us with this burden, so surely only he knows
how to make it bearable, because it is too heavy for us.

I am struck by the tranquil environment, completely opposite to the turmoil in my life. God's house is quiet, peaceful and soothing. I look out of the window, but time seems to have stood still . . . no traffic. My mind wanders back into the room and I watch my daughter's face again, as a silent frown creases her forehead. She has buried herself in the task at hand. I am not sure what she is painting, but it is keeping thoughts of the approaching cyclone at bay, at least for now.

My mind returns to the beginning of last year. Immediately, the image of my eldest daughter and her sister transforms the room, filling it with laughter, singing and dancing to Beyoncé. Nothing could dim their shared love of life and fun.

My daughters were both with child and due to give birth a few months apart. Big Sis was a mother-of-three, one daughter and two sons. She was now expecting another daughter, 'Like a magician, I have worked out a magic equation of two girls and two boys; isn't life just wonderful!' she used to say.

'Life is so wonderful! I can't believe that we are going to be mothers at the same time. You are the best motherhood teacher,' Little Sis would respond, as they hugged and kissed each other.

'Mum, can I play "My Girl" now?' I hear a soft voice drag me back into the present. Otis Redding is always the family music we play when we are happy or challenged. My daughter has finished her painting and seems to be getting restless. I nod my head and pause.

'Why don't you rest for a bit?' I say softly.

She doesn't answer but summons a version of 'My Girl'.

She comes to settle on the bean bag lying on my chest and I hug her as she sobs, at first quietly and then louder as her distress gains momentum. With each sob my heart is pierced, but I know that I must be strong for her. I want to wail, scream and lament to God, 'Why? Why? Dear Lord, why?' Instead, I shed deep silent tears drowning my heart. Did she really deserve this?

In the Bible Jacob mourns for his son's death, but I feel that the worst pain for any parent to endure is watching your child breaking and there is nothing you can do. That deep sense of helplessness strikes to the core.

My daughter had struggled with her pregnancy. She put her life in God's hands. She prayed for her unborn child. At twenty-nine weeks her doctor insisted that the baby had to be taken out or risk her own life, so the baby was born prematurely and stayed in hospital for ten weeks – ten long, scary weeks. My daughter never left her baby alone unless I came to take over for her to go home to rest. The baby was a fighter and a diva full of character, posing in the incubator as if she was at a beach with shades on. She was so funny.

'Mum, I can't breathe, I can't breathe!' A scream and coughing jolt me back again. I gently get up and get her some water. We carry out some breathing exercises together. When she is calm, I place her head on my lap and I stroke her hair gently. She starts dozing again. It's now 3:15 a.m. It's all calm and quiet now and once more my mind can wander.

After being home for six weeks, Baby Girl had gained weight to a normal size. We all relaxed.

Then one early morning, her mother and siblings found that Baby Girl had stopped breathing. They called an ambulance. The eldest child, a 13-year-old, was trying to resuscitate her sister the way the hospital had taught her till the ambulance crew took over. Three young siblings witnessed their distraught mother and the ambulance crew fighting to save their sister. Everyone was taken into the ambulance and they watched the paramedics, but they could not resuscitate her. My daughter was destroyed. 'Why, God, why?' She had fought to keep her baby, only to lose her just when she thought she was safe.

'Mum, when she was in hospital, I prepared myself to lose her, but once she was home, I relaxed and thought the worst was over. How can God be so cruel?'

I could not comfort her with an answer because I too was echoing the same feelings. Why? Why now?

I collected my daughter and her children to come and live with us, but that too was so difficult and painful. My younger daughter lived with us, and when her baby son cried, everyone was on edge, and he would be carried out of earshot to avoid reminding my elder daughter of her Baby Girl.

The two sisters had planned a double christening and had bought the babies matching outfits and ordered cakes for each baby. Baby Girl died two weeks before their christening. Some of the family are Roman Catholic, and Roman Catholics baptise babies from birth, so we were heartbroken that Baby Girl died before her planned baptism. We couldn't reconcile it and became angrier with God for tricking us to think that she had time to be baptised. How does a family cope with one deceased child and one living child? I didn't know what to do, and I prayed for wisdom. We later decided that we would have the funeral and the baptism on the same day. The last thing the two babies would do together.

The night before the funeral, my daughter did not want her baby to spend her last night on earth on her own, so we brought her home. First, we took her to a special service arranged by our Baptist church. We found the Baptist church comforting because children do not get baptised until they are old enough to make that decision themselves.

Baby Girl taught us a very difficult lesson on how to balance loss and celebration at the same time, which was captured by having her funeral on the same day as Baby Boy's christening.

My eldest daughter is still angry with God, but I pray that one day the wound will heal. My younger daughter developed a fear of Sudden Infant Death Syndrome (cot death) and is scared to have another baby in case he/she does not survive.

Back in the prayer room, my daughter is still on my lap. She raises her head and, half-asleep, whispers, 'We've made it. It's morning.'

'Yes,' I whisper back. No point in looking too far; just for now, this is good enough. We have survived the cyclone – her first anniversary.

'Sweet dreams, angel.'

Reflecting on the Bible account: Reuben's story

I told them it was wrong. I really tried. Yet, still I feel responsible. Even now as we look back, our family reunited, if I wake in the night, I experience again the rising shame, hot through my body. I wonder if I will ever be able to let it go.

It is hard being the eldest, and harder still when you know your father does not love your mother. Rachel, not Leah, was always his first love, and we all knew it. My brothers and I always sensed that we would never be as special to our father as Joseph and Benjamin, especially Joseph. That wretched coat! I thought that all the strutting around and those peculiar dreams were just coming from his own adolescent insecurities. I was wrong, as it turned out. But the others just got more and more enraged, jealousy for our father's affection eating away at all our souls.

Then came that fateful day. We were grazing our father's flocks in a valley near Dothan, further north than our home at Hebron and with more rain and better pasture. Joseph was not there. I couldn't work out if that was because he was too young or whether our father was sick of him whining about us bickering. Either way, I was enjoying some peace and quiet. Then suddenly in the distance we saw him, the familiar irritating swagger, the way he had of making you feel he was important, more important than you. My heart sank, but I never expected what would happen next. My brothers, their exasperation erupting into full-blown fury, decided to kill him and throw him in a cistern where time and rainwater would eventually cover any trace of what we had done.

I was horrified. I didn't like him either, but murder him? What would that do to our father? What would our God do to us? My brain was in a frenzy, but with my brothers baying for blood like a pack of wolves, all I could do was suggest we didn't kill him ourselves but just throw him in a pit. They would assume he would die, but I could rescue him later and hopefully by then their bloodlust would have subsided.

Well, of course, it all went horribly wrong. I'd gone off to check on some sheep which had wandered off, and I got back to find he was gone, sold to passing Arabs for a pittance. I was distraught, but there was no going back now. We killed a goat, and presented Joseph's bloody coat to our father, who assumed, just as we planned, that his precious son had been killed by an animal.

I can never forget my father's face that day, or in the days ahead. It was as if it was him, not Joseph, who was drained of life and vitality. He was suddenly grey and old in a way I had never seen him before. He stopped laughing. He would look into the distance as if remembering, and then his eyes, now dull, would fill with tears, overflowing down his cheeks. Worse still, sometimes his body would be racked with sobs, his head in his hands. At first we tried to comfort him, but when it was clear he was inconsolable, we stopped trying. I tried to avoid him, guilt pangs adding to my own misery, the lie sitting between us, a silent barrier. If ever we had doubted how important Joseph was to our father, it was clearer than ever now, but I for one would have preferred him back to the pall of desolation that hung in the air of the silent tent like a fog which no sun could disperse.

The years passed, and nothing changed. Then the famine hit, and now we found ourselves not just miserable but starving. So the ten of us set out for Egypt – having lost Joseph, there was no way Benjamin, the other son of my father's beloved Rachel, would be allowed anywhere. It was a long trek, and we arrived, bowing to ingratiate ourselves, to find a belligerent Egyptian in charge of the grain. Or so we thought. For three days we were imprisoned and in fear, accused of spying. We tried to communicate through the interpreter, but the allegations continued. I was beside myself. Surely this was judgement. I had tried to warn them! I could not read this man – at one point he turned away, and as he looked back his eyes were red. I had no idea why.

But we were desperate, so when he took Simeon and bound him, we still had to return home with the grain, knowing that our families were depending on us. Our fear grew to terror when we found our payment was still in the sacks of grain. How would we ever get Simeon back when as well as spies, this man would think we were thieves?

The famine continued, and again the grain ran out. A kind of resigned helplessness seemed to have settled over our father, and in the end, he sent us all, even Benjamin. Laden with gifts for this mysterious man, I could not even bear to look back at my father as we left. On arrival, we found ourselves being taken to the man's house, dreading the repercussions from our first visit. However, we were treated with kindness; by this time, we were exhausted by the journey and by our complex emotions, and profoundly confused. We presented Benjamin, and the grain master mysteriously disappeared, returning only to order his servants to serve the food, sitting at a distance because our races never mix. Bizarrely, Benjamin got far more to eat than us.

Off we went again, just wanting to get home, when suddenly we were overtaken and accused of stealing a special cup. When they found it in Benjamin's sack, I lost all hope myself, and on our return to face judgement, I had no words left. Judah spoke for all of us, though, telling again our version of Joseph's death and the importance of Benjamin to our father. Judah was noble, shaming us all by offering to stay instead if Benjamin was released.

And then it happened. He sent his servants away, and broke down, words tumbling out between sobs. He was Joseph. We did not believe him at first, he was so changed, but then slowly each of us realised it was true. He sobbed over Benjamin; he sobbed over us.

I wish I could say that reconciliation was complete, that I felt forgiven, and all was well. It is never that simple, though, is it? Our father and our families joined us, we were given land, and all was good. Yet all of us lived fearing the future. That once our father died, old resentments would rise, and in the end, we would face the punishment we undoubtedly deserved.

That is not what happened, though. Turned out Joseph was a bigger man than all of us. After our father's funeral he simply wept further, and told us that God had turned what we did to good.

I'm left wondering, though. What if I had insisted all those years ago that we treated him well? What then? And who is this God, who takes such murderous rage and uses it to bring life?

(The story of Joseph and his brothers is told in Genesis 29, 37 and 39 – 50.)

The quotation at the start of this chapter records the words of Jacob, the father of Joseph who is famed for his multicoloured coat, weeping because he has been tricked by his other sons into believing that Joseph is dead. There have been tears shed earlier in Jacob's story, not least in his reconciliation with his brother Esau after a long estrangement.[2] The story of Jacob's son Joseph and his brothers seems to have more instances of weeping than any other in the Bible. After the text at the start of the chapter, there are eight more examples, seven instances of Joseph weeping,[3] and one of Benjamin.[4] We can also safely assume there were times when other members in the family shed tears. This is a family in a world of pain.

Sometimes people say to me that the Bible is an outdated book, not relevant to life today with all of its complexity. Yet, looking at biblical families that is simply not the case, particularly in the Old Testament – they are as multifaceted as any today. Many Bible 'heroes', including Abraham, David and Jacob, had more than one wife, or a mix of wives and concubines – a kind of legal mistress. Biblical marriages were arranged, sometimes resembling a business transaction – which is partly what makes what we might consider love stories, such as that of Jacob and Rachel, stand out.[5] Much of the significance of marriage was connected to the provision of children, in particular male children (heirs) – hence the suggestion of Abram's wife Sarai[6] that he sleep with her Egyptian maid, a course of action with disastrous consequences. There are tragic stories of incest and abuse, such as the story of Tamar,[7] and of devastating bereavement, such as David's loss of his wives taken in war (albeit recovered), his baby son, and his adult son Absalom.[8]

Significant biblical figures of faith like Eli and David have children who do not share that faith or openly rebel.[9] These were not simpler days.

A variety of groups in society, including some Christian organisations, bewail the demise of the traditional family. Yet a 'traditional' family has a wide range of expressions in different cultures. In the Roman society which forms the backdrop to the Gospels and epistles, family life was dependent on slaves – perhaps as many as 60 million across the empire.[10] The '*paterfamilias*', or male head of the household, had absolute power, even to decide if a newborn baby should be allowed to live or die.[11] Family types across cultures can include two generational (adults and children), three generational (including, for example, grandparents), monogamous, polygamous, patriarchal, matriarchal, nuclear and extended.[12] Whilst the nuclear family, with its own variations (including same-sex couples, stepfamilies and single-parent families) might be the norm in the West, that is not the case globally.

Sometimes there is a specific call for a return to the 'biblical pattern' for family life.[13] These voices sometimes assume this pattern consists of two parents (one of each gender), with the male as the leader in the household, often with reference to the wife submitting.[14] Often these calls for a biblical pattern rest on scriptures such as 1 Corinthians 11:3: 'But I want you to realise that the head of every man is Christ, and the head of the woman is man, and the head of Christ is God.' This verse has been taken to be about leadership and authority, but its context is teaching on public worship, not family life, and there are other ways of interpreting this text and the very few other similar ones.[15] The biblical picture actually seems to be very fluid, and experience tells us that in the area of family life there are more greys than on any artist's palette.

Whatever the family pattern we or others might aspire to, or already possess, it is clear that families can be places of great joy, but also great pain, and for a wide variety of reasons, some of which we see in Joseph's story.

Difficulties began in this family with favouritism. Joseph was the first of two sons by his true love, Rachel, whose other son was Benjamin. Jacob unwisely singled Joseph out with the famous coat, and the adolescent Joseph did not help by repeating dreams which clearly implied that he would be superior to his brothers and his parents. These actions, presumably reflecting the general ethos of the family, were to have disastrous consequences. Sibling rivalry is a well-recognised reality, with an interesting parallel in nature with siblicide among some species of young birds when food is limited. A supremely honest book about human frailty, the Bible also relates the ultimate story of sibling rivalry in the killing of his brother Abel by Cain.[16] Some sibling issues, as here, are at least partially the result of unwise parenting, but can also be circumstantial – for example, because another of the children has major health issues which takes the time and attention of parents. Bias towards a particular child may also be a perception, no matter how scrupulous parents try to be in their fairness. There are variables in how children respond to favouritism, whether perceived or real, but it is undoubtedly one of the sources of family pain.

Estrangement between family members is also a source of great distress in families, whether it is between parents and children, between adult siblings, or in other relationships such as grandparents and grandchildren. Grandparents temporarily or even permanently losing contact with their grandchildren is one of the often unrecognised losses in divorce. An ex-husband or wife, who has been a member of the family, sometimes for years, usually loses touch with their ex-in-laws too, and this loss can be felt keenly if they had been loved as a full part of the family. For Joseph, the estrangement went very deep: his brothers initially plan to kill him, and then sell him as a slave. It is remarkable that reconciliation eventually occurs, given that their betrayal results in him being taken to Egypt and subsequently falsely accused of sexual misconduct and imprisoned. It is hardly surprising it is accompanied with a great deal of weeping on Joseph's part. I cannot help but wonder if those tears were mixed – relief and joy at the reconciliation, but also grief at all that has happened, which can only now be released.

Joseph is geographically separated from his family, not of his own choice, and therein lies another source of pain within families. I recently spoke with a lady who freely admitted that she finds the separation from her children almost unbearable as they reside in other continents because of their careers. Skype and FaceTime are certainly an improvement from previous generations, but the sense of loss when adult children move away is very deep. I have been hugely blessed by my daughter (and grandchildren) always living fairly near, but still remember the tears I wept leaving my son at university and realising that he was unlikely to ever live at home again. This loss due to geography is exacerbated if there are grandchildren, with whom it is difficult to build a relationship at a distance, and as the older generation become less mobile and travel to see their family becomes more difficult.

Sometimes, sadly, the pain from family life is because of profound neglect or abuse. When I worked as a counsellor, I heard many stories of childhoods which included experiences no child (or adult) should ever be subjected to and which inevitably left scars which went very deep. The things we see and hear and the way we are brought up are foundational to who we become and our view of ourselves and the world, especially if they are a repeated pattern, or occur at an age when we are particularly vulnerable.[17] It is possible to build new ways of seeing ourselves and the world and to manage the impact of those experiences, but my own view is that we cannot eradicate the results of our upbringings, merely ameliorate the effects.[18]

Loss of significant family members by death is another cause of great pain. Joseph's first recorded words when he finally chooses to reveal who he is to his brothers, in Egypt, are an anguished 'Is my father still living?'[19] Both my parents had died by the time I was 25, my father after a long illness and my mother suddenly, and I know those losses have both impacted me in different ways. I cannot begin to imagine the pain of losing a child and the agony of Bible characters who do, both men and women, is plain to see. Naomi, both of whose sons die, as well as her husband, responds with a bitterness born from grief. For Jacob, losing (as he believes) one son of his beloved Rachel means he is protective about her other son.

Another source of family pain is wanting a family but not being able to have one. This ongoing ache is not helped by social media, where on the whole the only pictures posted are happy scenes with smiling faces, or expressions of family pride. It seems to me that one of the key – and perhaps underestimated – messages of the life of Jesus is that God has identified with the anguish of human families in the most intimate of ways. He is born into a family which has experienced unjustified scandal because of a pregnancy resulting (supposedly) from infidelity, a family which then experiences great fear and displacement as refugees. As far as we can tell, Jesus then at some point before adulthood experiences the death of a parent, his father Joseph. There are clear indications that he is misunderstood and rejected by at least some of his siblings,[20] though James at least later changed his mind and was one of the leaders in the early church.[21] Mary has the excruciating agony of watching her son die in the most humiliating and painful way. Jesus' own family knew great pain.

The Bible uses the image of the church as a family, children of the Father and siblings to Jesus and to each other.[22] At times the church can bring its own form of family pain in equally varied ways, through judgementalism, or even, tragically, abuse of various kinds.[23] However, at its best the church can be a place where we can find a degree of healing from pain experienced in our original families. Having lost my father when I was 12, I have learned a great deal from father figures in the church. Churches can be incredibly supportive to families who are struggling, whether in practical help or through the equally important day-to-day acceptance, listening, encouragement and prayer.

Some questions to reflect on

- Are there any of the kinds of pain that Joseph's family encountered that you can identify with?
- What are the kinds of pain that you have seen in those around you in their families? How have you tried to help and support them?
- What kinds of help can, or should, the local church give to families experiencing difficulties?
- Are there any aspects of your own experience of family, past or present, which are still difficult? What kinds of support might you find helpful and how can you find it?

3

Tears at Goodbyes

*Then Naomi said to her two daughters-in-law,
'Go back, each of you, to your mother's home.
May the LORD show you kindness, as you have
shown kindness to your dead husbands and to
me. May the LORD grant that each of you will
find rest in the home of another husband.' Then
she kissed them goodbye and they wept aloud and
said to her, 'We will go back with you to your
people.'*[1]

A current story of tears at goodbyes

We were standing in the hallway of my Edwardian home. My
eyes were looking down, trying to concentrate on the blue and
cream striped wallpaper under the new dado rail to keep my
emotions under control, but I could tell that my resolve not to
cry was weakening.

I think we are all different in our patterns of friendship, and
I have always been someone who forms a few, deep friendships
which are very important to me. It takes me a while to open up
and trust people, and so once that is established, I feel it deeply

if the relationship is lost. Friendships are built in a myriad of ways, and the one threatening to bring me to tears that day, as is often the case, had started in the workplace. At the time I was running a counselling service, with more than twenty volunteers, but I had bonded particularly well with one of them, as apart from the work we had shared interests, both in creative forms of worship and in birdwatching. We had confided in one another about our respective histories and enjoyed many relaxed cups of coffee, alternating easily between humorous banter and deep discussions on many topics.

But now the tears threatened to tumble unbidden, coursing down my cheeks. My friend was moving away, and I was struggling with this final goodbye. In contrast, she was quite rational – we would still see each other, it was only a couple of hours away, we could still visit sometimes. Yet I knew this move would change the nature of our friendship – phone calls are never the same as leisurely conversations over coffee, and I would miss the closeness and mutual empathy we had developed. I recognised that for her it was different – she was moving on to new and exciting things. The gap caused by the loss of our easy mutual understanding would soon be filled with new friends. For me, however, things would continue the same, and so I would feel the loss more keenly.

And so, as we hugged as she left, we both wept, but I wept the most.

Reflecting on the Bible account: Naomi's story

Not another goodbye. My soul is aching with goodbyes. My whole life has been governed by them, and they are eating away at me like vultures feeding on a rotting corpse.

The first was years ago now. Famine had hit us, as it so often does. There was barely enough to feed my sons: Mahlon the older one living on husks, Kilion the younger one sucking hopelessly at my breasts where the milk was drying up. Then one day Elimelech came to me, sorrow in his eyes, to tell me that we had to leave. At first I protested. 'There must be another way?' How could I leave all that was familiar: the women in the village with whom I had shared the pregnancies and birth stories, who I had drawn water alongside, and who had cried and laughed with me. But in the end I knew, watching the drawn cheeks of my sons, that he was right, and so, weeping, I waved goodbye to everything that was familiar, trudging wearily but with resolute determination to my new life in Moab.

For a while it was bearable – at least the children were fed, though I balked at the different traditions and felt very alone. But then my husband got sick. I watched him change day by day, his flesh hanging where once he had been strong and muscular. One day, as I nursed him, he caught hold of my hand. 'Take care of the boys,' he said, his voice somehow resonating with defeat. I opened my mouth to protest, but he raised his finger to my lips to silence my meaningless reassurance. We looked at each other, understanding that this was goodbye, and I knew that I had to let him go. That evening he was gone, slipping away into the darkness of death.

My boys kept me going. I gleaned grain, cleaned and sowed garments, and people were kind. The next goodbyes should have been joyful, I suppose: said at the weddings of my sons, leaving me for their new lives. In one way they were, and my happiness was real, but in another way, I felt I had lost them too, and again I wept, joy and sadness intermingled. I was alone, and thought time and again of all that I had left behind in my home village. But my sons were here, and I could not leave them.

But then they left me. First one, and then the other. I stood at each of their graves, only memories left, and what good was reminiscing to me now? This time the tears were absent, dried up like my womb and breasts, as arid as my hope for anything good to ever happen in my life again. I said goodbye to my two boys and, with them, to my future. I would not sit grandchildren on my lap like the other women. There was nothing left for me here, or anywhere.

Home. That was all I wanted now. To say farewell to this land which had ripped everything from me. To let the women back in Bethlehem hold me in my grief at all I had lost, just as once they held me as my sons entered the world. There was food there now, the famine ended, and I knew I must leave.

And so here we were, my meagre possessions wrapped on the donkey I'd been given, on this dusty road. Orpah and Ruth, my son's widows, were with me, and at first I assumed they were coming just to wave to me as I departed at the edge of the village. But then I realised they intended to come. 'No, no,' I said. 'You need to stay here, with your own people. You have been kind to me, perhaps God will be kind to you.' A hollow hope, but one I felt I had to express. They had suffered too, though I had nothing left with which to see past my own pain to comfort them.

They tried to insist, but this time I was determined there would be a farewell, no matter how much I wanted them to stay with me to, however minimally, assuage the loneliness that was suffocating me like the shrouds I had placed over those I loved. What could I offer them? They needed a future, and I had none.

So Orpah left me, and I thought no worse of her for that. We kissed, and cried, and she was gone.

But Ruth, ah, she would not say goodbye. That was one leave-taking that was not going to happen.

And so we set off for Bethlehem, with no idea what would await us there.

(Naomi's story is found throughout the book of Ruth: this section is based on Ruth 1.)

I really don't like goodbyes. I never have, and it never gets any better. I realise none of us do, but I find them particularly painful. I can rationalise why – when I was just 12, I lost my father, my grandmother, my home and my beloved dog (who was put down because of the move and changed circumstances) all in the space of a couple of months. That is a pretty catastrophic collection of losses at a young age, and has left its legacy, particularly as there was no opportunity to say goodbye to any of them, apart from my home. As a result, it is very important to me to say goodbye, even if the person is only going away for a week or two. When someone I care for is dying, it matters to me a great deal to be able to say goodbye in some way – whatever is appropriate for them – but it wrenches my heart out every time.

There are a number of biblical farewells, of various kinds. Laban berates his son-in-law Jacob, who has run from him, for not allowing him to say goodbye to his daughters and grandchildren, although he is later able to do so.[2] Moses and Jethro, his father-in-law, part company, Jethro returning home and Moses heading towards the Promised Land.[3] Elisha is allowed to say goodbye to his family as he heads off with his mentor Elijah.[4] Jesus warns of the need to say goodbye to some things to follow him.[5] The apostle Paul had several occasions of needing to leave people as he travelled, and a particularly emotional farewell to the Ephesians.[6] As we saw in the story above, Naomi endured several goodbyes, including a move and three significant deaths.

Goodbyes come in various forms, but for most of us the goodbyes we say to people are the hardest. Relationships are key to our wellbeing as people. As John Donne famously said, no man (and, of course, it is equally true of women) is an island.[7] Sometimes Christian teaching or the lyrics of worship songs can imply that all we need is God, however, one of the ways we experience the care of God is from each other – what I refer to as 'God with skin on'.[8] Mutual dependence is an important part of our humanity, and will vary in its form at different stages of our lives, such as a parent initially caring for their child, and then in turn being cared for by them in their later years.[9] This need for each other is one of the reasons that we struggle with saying goodbye. We are made for connection, and so when a connection is lost, it threatens our sense of security and even of self – we can feel as though a part of us has been lost too. Whilst I do believe that we are created primarily for connection with God, how we experience that is hugely impacted by our experiences with others, particularly early in our lives.

Those who have studied attachment theory, such as John Bowlby, have had some very helpful things to say in this area. As babies we are completely dependent on our carers for survival, and so, if we are looked after well, the bond is strong. As we grow, a child learns that they can manage small separations from their primary carer, as long as the substitute care is good, and that both the length of separation, and the way it is handled, are age appropriate. When my children were small and I first left them with other people, I was told to simply slip away while they were playing. However, I felt it was important that they knew I was leaving, as then they could experience that I went away, but would come back. If they were old enough for me to explain to them, they could also learn that what I said could be trusted. Erik Erikson, a German-American developmental psychologist and psychoanalyst, has been very influential in our understanding of how we develop from childhood through to adulthood. He describes the first stage of that development, covering roughly the first eighteen months of life, as being the time when an infant acquires a sense of basic trust, of confidence in caregivers and in the world in general as opposed to a view of the world based on anxiety and fear if care is inadequate.[10]

How our attachments develop, and whether they are disrupted, for example by an erratic pattern of caregivers or significant ill-health of the child or carers, has huge implications for our mental health and many aspects of the way we experience and respond to life. One of those features is our sensitivity to goodbyes. There are, of course, many different kinds of goodbyes we say to people, not least in terms of their permanence. We would normally not expect to be as distressed by saying goodbye to a work colleague who is going away for two weeks as by the departure of someone who is emigrating, for example. However, our emotional reactions are rarely straightforward. We can experience one situation 'as if'[11] it is another one which is triggered in our memory, often unconsciously. If our reactions seem excessive or unexpected, it may help to ask ourselves whether there is an echo of another situation that may be impacting us. We will also have been influenced by the patterns we experienced in our family of origin. My mother was brought up in an orphanage and struggled with expressing her emotions. When my father was dying, she hid it from me, and I was excluded from his funeral. This was well-intentioned but ultimately unhelpful, and I suspect was partly from her own difficulty, which I saw at various times, with any form of goodbye.

Goodbyes may be chosen or imposed, and that makes a difference to the way that we respond. In the story at the start of the chapter, the two people responded differently because one had chosen to leave and the other had no choice in the goodbye. Even when it is our choice, we may still be sad, but it is different from a situation which is imposed. The less control we have, the more likely we are to experience feelings of helplessness or even anger, as emotions from when we were small are evoked. Whether we choose an ending or not, it is still important to allow ourselves the mix of feelings rather than just immerse ourselves in the changed situation.

It is important to recognise that it is not always sadness that we experience when leaving a situation or person. At times, where there has been conflict, for example, it may be a relief to say goodbye. This reaction can also be part of our response when someone has died and can be difficult to acknowledge. At other times we may need a goodbye to move on to something positive – such as leaving one job to start another, or ending counselling after we have been helped. It is healthy if we can allow ourselves a wide range of emotions and find a way to accept them rather than repress them.

Over time, we develop patterns of dealing with goodbyes, particularly if there have been difficult goodbyes in the past. Some people do everything to try to avoid them, even boycotting the funerals of the people close to them. Others will leave a relationship before they can be left. One person I knew, faced with a counsellor they had begun to trust seeking to set an ending to their sessions, simply left the next time they were due to meet. Whilst far from ideal, she recognised that she was choosing to take back control as there were a number of very difficult losses she had experienced in the past over which she had no control. Sometimes, to try to make a goodbye bearable, people minimise the importance of the relationship, either to themselves or others. Of course, the only way to prevent saying goodbye altogether is to never engage in relationships at all – a lonely but understandable reaction to painful experiences in the past. Counselling can be really helpful when goodbyes are very difficult, for example by allowing us to explore in that safe space our feelings about relationships, hopefully ending the counselling in a planned way, and perhaps finding a different way to say goodbye.

A helpful goodbye may be laced with tears, but also gives us the opportunity to celebrate what was good about our relationship with that person, or about the situation we are leaving, to laugh as well as cry, and even to forgive if that is needed. When I left the first church I had served in, and where I had been a member for thirty-eight years and worked for twenty-eight, we devised what we termed 'release prayers'. They celebrated the good that I had received from the church and the church from my ministry. They also asked and offered forgiveness for any ways I had, inevitably, failed the church and ways they had failed me. Finally, they released me from my responsibilities there to free me to move on to the next stage of ministry. It was very emotional, with tears on all sides, but felt a very healthy part of what was, because of my deep roots there, a very difficult goodbye.

Some questions to reflect on

- What is your earliest memory of saying goodbye?
- Are there any particular kinds of goodbye you find especially difficult? Can you work out why that might be?
- What is your pattern of saying goodbye?
- Can you take anything from this chapter which might help you the next time you face a goodbye?

4

Tears of Friendship

David got up . . . and bowed down before Jon-
athan three times, with his face to the ground.
Then they kissed each other and wept to-
gether – but David wept the most.[1]

A current story of tears of friendship

It was a familiar scene. Parking my car, I made my way into the
hospice through the rain, my hood shielding me from the driz-
zle but not from the sadness and anxiety at the daunting task
that lay ahead. It is a journey which as a minister I make many
times, and it is never easy. So often there are no words and I
know all I can offer is a quiet presence, perhaps a hand to hold,
and to be someone who will listen to anything – especially
words which can be too hard for those I visit to say to anyone
else. Seriously ill and dying people often protect those nearest
to them from their fears and other deep feelings, not wanting
to add to the distress of their families and friends. So, I know
that it may be really important to listen to the fear, anger or
despair. Each time I leave the encounter with a heavy heart, but
aware too that it is a great honour that I can be there.

But this was different. This was my friend. We had laughed together, shared secrets, put the world to rights over coffee. Our conversations had ranged from the trivial to the profound, sharing faith and moments of doubt and knowing both would be held lightly and with love.

But right now, she needed me to be a minister. To read God's Word, pray, to offer hope and assurance. To somehow represent God's presence in the very darkest moments. Praying that I could hold it together, I did the best I could, said goodbye knowing this might well be the last time I would see her, and walked from the room, looking behind me only to blow her a kiss.

I knew I could not just go back out into the cold November evening. So, I went to find the chapel, unsure if I wanted someone there or not. It was empty and quiet, and so I sat in wordless prayer, and with relief at last allowed the tears to flow. Tears of sorrow, for those she loved. Tears of frustration at this wretched disease which was robbing her of vitality and would soon steal her life.

But most of all, tears because she was my friend.

Reflecting on the Bible account: David's story

Mephibosheth arrived in court today. Poor, crippled Mephibosheth. Saul's grandson. Jonathan's son. He bowed before me, revealing with his eyes as much as with his body that his spirit was as crushed as his legs, something I saw even more painfully in his description of himself as a 'dead dog'.[2] I could barely imagine the abject terror as he and his nurse had run for their lives,[3] hearing the news that Saul and Jonathan were dead. Finally, he raised his face and as I fully met his gaze, I saw his father, my closest friend, reflected in it.

I'm going to do the right thing. Mephibosheth will be welcomed in court and provided for, his days of exile at an end. My advisors think I'm foolhardy – that I should kill anyone who is related to Saul and so might pose a threat to my throne. They might be right, but this is Jonathan's son. I cannot harm him.

So now, the court dismissed, I sit quite alone, as all the memories come flooding back, a curious mix of aching sadness and loving gratitude. My friend Jonathan. The best friend a man could ever have.

I'd heard of him of course, before we encountered each other. His exploits were the talk of the Israelite camp, a worthy successor-in-waiting for the kingship still held by his father, Saul. Yet the day we met, as we instinctively embraced as brothers, I somehow knew that power meant nothing to him and loyalty everything. He simply had no need for the adulation I was to discover his father so disastrously craved. We made a covenant that day, binding ourselves to each other for all that lay ahead. As he passed me his robe, tunic, sword, bow and belt I sensed that Jonathan was laying down so much more than that – setting aside his own future to serve the one God seemed to have mapped out for me. Our mutual trust was instinctive, but it would be sorely tested in the days ahead.

And then one day as I played the harp, as if from nowhere Saul's spear hit the wall, and as I looked up in shock, I saw the hatred in his eyes. It was eating him up, consuming him from the inside like a fire, which my mere existence seemed to fuel. I saw fear, too, despite the family bond we shared through Michal's love for me. From that day on I still tried to serve him faithfully but nothing helped, and my playing, which had so soothed him, now seemed to have lost its power to heal either the growing rift between us or the maelstrom of bitter loathing within him.

When Jonathan sought me out to warn me of the latest plot, I could see the pain and distress in his eyes. Torn between his love for his father and for me – as he would be to the end of his days – he chose friendship over family, risking his father's displeasure to speak well of me. Then came the New Moon festival when again he saved my life, but we knew the die was cast and I could not stay any longer. My soul startled as I heard him say – half a hope and half a prayer – 'May the LORD be with you as he has been with my father'.[4] Because he said 'has been' – past tense. Jonathan saw with his characteristic perception that Saul had passed the point of no return . . . with me but, far more tragically, with God. The darkness had engulfed him.

And so I wept as Jonathan and I parted. They were mixed tears, I can see in retrospect – some self-pity for my impending exile with all its uncertainty mingling with the sadness of our farewell. Jonathan cried too, but I could feel his resolve, his willingness to sacrifice his longing to cling to our companionship because of his greater desire both for my safety and for me to become all God intended. Neither of us knew it then, but we were to meet just one more time, when he sought me out to encourage me, before he lost his life in battle and I lost the greatest friend I ever had.

Jonathan. Oh, Jonathan. Carrying the heavy responsibility of the kingship as I do now, how different it would have been if you had lived. If I have learned anything about how to be a friend, it was from you. So now I remember, and I weep again.

(The story of the friendship between Jonathan and David is found particularly in 1 Samuel 18 – 20, 1 Samuel 23:16–18 and 2 Samuel 9.)

Friendship is one of the defining characteristics of our lives. Many parents worry as much about the friendships of their children as their academic achievement, and I believe rightly so. Our friendships hold great capacity for growth and harm, protection and betrayal. They impact our development as people in profound and long-lasting ways.

Children's literature, from the earliest books children look at or read (as well as the now inevitable linked TV shows or films), are full of friendships. Winnie-the-Pooh and his friends accept the variety of personalities in their midst, from the irrepressible Tigger to Eeyore, who even in his dark moods is looked after by them all, even the rather supercilious owl. Some friendships are unlikely – who could have imagined that a spider and pig would become friends, as in *Charlotte's Web*? In some books, the friendships result in profound life-changing experiences for one or more characters, such as for Sophie and the BFG. More recently, undoubtedly one of the factors in the phenomenal success of the Harry Potter books is the unshakeable friendship between Harry, Ron and Hermione. For an older market and in a different medium, one of the most watched television series of all time, lasting ten series and aired from 1994 to 2004 but still frequently repeated is entitled simply *F.R.I.E.N.D.S* and charts the complex relationships of a group of friends with a very deep bond.

My personal all-time favourite films of *The Hobbit*[5] and *The Lord of the Rings*[6] both have friendship as a central theme, as do the books they are based on. In the film of *The Hobbit* Bilbo is betrayed and misunderstood by the troubled Thorin Oakenshield, yet when asked towards the end of the third film, after Thorin's death, who this Thorin is, he replies poignantly about their friendship, making no reference to their many difficulties. In *The Lord of the Rings*, the unsung hero is in many ways Sam, who accompanies Frodo on his quest to destroy the ring, and without whom it would have ended in disaster. Their friendship also survives misunderstanding, and the book includes other important bonds, such as the one between Merry and Pippin and even, surprisingly, between the elf Legolas and the dwarf Gimli whose respective cultures had long-standing enmity. Cast your mind to your own favourite songs, books and films and you may be surprised how frequently friendship is at their heart.

There are many factors that exist in the creation and maintaining of friendships, not least simple proximity. In playgroups and schools we are surrounded by others with whom we share mutual experiences, and playing together makes for a ready bond, whilst parents frequently form friendships at the school gates. Later, work or social activities often lead to friendships, as do activities based on mutual values, such as in a faith community. In later life it is perhaps more difficult, as working life ends and children are grown. This, together with the loss of contact with friends through immobility and death, is one of the contributing factors to loneliness in older people. However, although developing a new friendship is sometimes due to people possessing similar ages or life experiences, it is not always the case. A young woman in our congregation shared a friendship with a gentleman in his nineties which was precious to them both, and she felt his loss keenly when he died, speaking movingly at his funeral.

Sometimes we simply do not know what draws us into friendship. David and Jonathan's friendship appears to have started after David kills the Philistine giant Goliath.[7] Saul enquires who he is, David answers, and the bond is described in this way: 'After David had finished talking with Saul, Jonathan became one in spirit with David, and he loved him as himself.'[8] We cannot help but wonder what birthed their friendship. Certainly, both are brave men – Jonathan defeated a garrison of Philistines at Geba[9] and with his armour bearer left Saul's army at Gebeah and captured the outpost at Michmash.[10] Later events also prove they are people of principle – both honouring their friendship and David refusing to kill King Saul even when the opportunity arises.[11]

Among many other things, friendships are, it seems to me, rather like an oasis, a place of safety when things become difficult. To this day there are two friends who I would want to see, or at least contact, in the darkest times. One I share a friendship with that has spanned five decades, the other at least three. There is a sense of shared history, of not needing to explain myself, of mutual acceptance which runs very deep. Other friendships, less long-lasting, have been that same shelter in specific times, and whilst the relationships might not have lasted as long, I carry those people in my heart with gratitude.

For David and Jonathan, that aspect of safety was literal as well as metaphorical. King Saul, Jonathan's father and David's king, had begun by admiring David, taking him into the court, and being soothed by his music. However, as the king's insecurity and paranoia grew, this turned to hostility. An initial, seemingly impulsive attack on David, hurling a spear as he (ironically) played to soothe Saul, turned into full enmity as Saul ordered both his servants and his son to kill David. Jonathan both warned David and spoke to his father on his behalf, brokering a temporary reconciliation. However, Saul later reneged and David again became a fugitive. He sought out Jonathan for help. They came up with an elaborate plan for Jonathan to ascertain the risk to David and either encourage him back or warn him to leave. Saul was implacable, Jonathan alerted David, and they both wept as they said goodbye. Jonathan had saved his friend's life and throughout the story this friendship stands in sharp contrast to the hatred of Saul.

However it may begin, for something to be truly friendship, it has to be mutual. Some relationships of genuine caring – such as in counselling or pastoral work – are very important, but lack the mutuality of real friendship, although this can be mis-understood by the recipients of that care.[12] The biblical pic-ture of the relationship between David and Jonathan is that of a covenant.[13] A covenant – not a word we use as much now – is a binding agreement or promise between two people or groups. At one point in David and Jonathan's story, they reaffirm their commitment because Jonathan 'loved him as he loved himself'.[14] In Hebrew and Greek the words for friend-ship and love are linked.[15] Love biblically is not just (or even primarily) an emotion, but involves heart, soul and strength.[16] Determination and action are involved. Aristotle described three types of friendship – based on pleasure (enjoying a com-mon activity), usefulness (neighbours or business associates helping each other), or virtue (loving someone for the qualities they possess and seeking the good of the other).[17] This last kind he considered superior, and certainly it is those qualities that Jonathan demonstrated.

Friendship also involves seeing the best in someone. Jonathan saw that God had a plan for David. In close friendships we will, of course, see the frailty in the other, any moments of selfish-ness, the things that are not the best. Yet we hopefully decide instead to focus on the good, and where necessary to defend the other person when others choose to emphasise the worst. When a friend experiences times of insecurity or doubt, we may need to remind them of the good qualities that we see. Most of us are our own harshest critics, seeing ourselves in a distorted mirror like those in old-fashioned fairgrounds. We need people who see us realistically, and also with kindness, who can tell us things that we have either never realised or have forgotten about ourselves. We are impoverished if we don't have those who will cheer us on when we are about to give up, but who equally will challenge us to be our best when we are in danger of taking a wrong turn.

Friendship at times can be costly. This may be as simple as inconvenience – the friend who wants to stay when we were looking forward to a quiet weekend, or who needs us to listen when we are tired or distracted ourselves. Or it may involve much more. His friendship with David was costly to Jonathan, invoking his father's anger against him. Such was his commitment to David that he was prepared to put his own right to be king aside to see David crowned and to serve him – although because of his death this was never possible, his willingness to do so was indicative that he was prepared to sacrifice himself for his friend.[18]

My favourite portion in this moving story takes place when Jonathan came to find David, still on the run, at Horesh. The sense of the text is that David, unsurprisingly, was tired and fearful, something we know from the Psalms.[19] Jonathan sought him out. This proactive care can be very important. Sometimes we cannot reach out for the help that we need, but need to be sought out.

When I was very small, I often hid in places: notably under the stairs or beneath a large camellia bush in our garden. Actually, at those times I did not want to be found, but as a result, developed the habit of hiding in other less literal ways, which have not always served me well. At times I have needed someone to seek me out – to not just accept the reflex 'I'm fine' but to care enough to ask if that was really true, check out if my silence by email or calls might indicate more than simply a busy spell, and persist if initially batted away.

Having sought David out, it is beautifully expressed that Jonathan 'helped him to find strength in God'.[20] When things are tough, one of the most helpful ways we can be there for each other is by prayer and support spiritually. By that I do not mean tossing Scripture verses at someone like a harried doctor reaching prematurely for the prescription pad. I mean holding on to hope for our friend, keeping praying, hearing the questions and the pain, and trusting that God is faithful and will somehow hold them in the darkness, doing so including and perhaps especially through us. I hope I have been able to do that for others, and certainly friends have done that for me, which has undoubtedly kept me not just in the church but, more importantly, able to somehow hang on to belief in God in the most difficult of times.

The tears shed when the two men said their first goodbye were not to be the last for David. Several years after his last recorded meeting at Horesh, the Israelites are again engaged in battle with their old enemies the Philistines. Three of Saul's sons, including Jonathan, are killed in battle and Saul also dies.[21] News reaches David, who has been engaged in a separate battle. He and his men tore their clothes – an expression of grief, as in those times clothes were among the most treasured of people's possessions. Then they 'mourned and wept . . . for Saul and his son Jonathan'.[22] The loss of a friend, whether by a breakdown in relationship, geographical distance or death, is one of the most painful (and often underestimated) bereavements that we will suffer. It is a risk we take for any kind of love, friendship included.

Jesus had very mixed experiences with his own friends, the disciples. Peter misunderstood it when Jesus indicated that he was going to die, and tried to argue him out of it.[23] Later he denied even knowing Jesus.[24] It appears most of the disciples scattered after Jesus was arrested, with only John being recorded at the crucifixion.[25] Part of the evidence for the resurrection is that their rather patchy loyalty became so strong after Jesus was raised from the dead that, in contrast with earlier, they were prepared to die rather than deny him.

One of the biblical images for our relationship with God is friendship. Despite their inconsistency, Jesus says to his disciples, and so to us: 'I no longer call you servants, because a servant does not know his master's business. Instead, I have called you friends, for everything that I learned from my Father I have made known to you.'[26] Like other friendships, the one with God starts in many ways, develops over time, takes work, time and energy, and changes us. It is a friendship made possible only by God's relentless love for us, and as indispensable as the other friendships I have had and do have are, for me it has been and is the most transformative of them all.

Some questions to reflect on

- Look back at one of your long-lasting friendships. How did it start? What has kept it going?
- Think about some friendships that have not stood the test of time. What contributed to them not lasting?

- How can you be better at being someone who helps others find strength in God? Is there anyone just now who needs your support in that way? Or if you need it yourself at the moment, where are the places you might be helped to find it?
- What might thinking about your relationship with God as friendship add to your understanding of the spiritual life?

5

Tears of Loss

*While the child was still alive, I fasted and wept
. . . but now that he is dead, why should I go on
fasting?*[1]

*The king was shaken. He went up to the room
over the gateway and wept. As he went, he said:
'O my son Absalom! My son, my son Absalom! If
only I had died instead of you – O Absalom, my
son, my son!'*[2]

A current story of tears of loss

It was the day I had dreaded. Our beloved dog, who had been a
faithful companion for sixteen years, was dying. I knew we had
to make one of the most painful choices of our lives and help
ease her suffering, and the vet, herself fond of her, was coming
to the house to save her the trauma of a last visit to the surgery,
surrounded by other dogs who intimidated her and breathing
in the smell she had always hated. The night before she had
slept on my bed, so that I could put my arm on her, reassuring
her I was there. I knew she was aware of something in the air in

the uncanny way dogs are. Other members of the family had said their tearful goodbyes.

The doorbell rang. Trusting as ever, she ran to the door, ready to welcome whoever might be there, and greeted the vet like an old friend, tail wagging. She had loved people all her life with that wonderful ability to be open to all that few of us humans possess. I tried to hold myself together, to not distress her in those last moments. And then I sat and held her, stroked her, and thanked her for all the years that had brought us all such joy. With great kindness the vet did what she had to do, and my beloved dog slipped away in my arms. I just managed to let the vet out, as she gently cradled my beloved dog's body to take her to the crematorium, and then, the house so silent, I wept.

As you read this, you may have one of two reactions. One will be incredulity – it is 'just a dog, it is humans that matter' – which of course they do. Or, if you have had a much-loved pet, you will understand that they are very much a part of the family, that they offer such sweet, unconditional acceptance, seem somehow to understand when we weep into their fur, even curling around us without us saying a word when we are distressed.

But that day my grief was cumulative. So yes, I cried for her, unashamedly, and wept again in writing these words. But her loss, as every other, built on each one that had gone before and the tears were indivisible. So, I was crying too for my father, who died after a long illness when I was 12 and from whose funeral I had been excluded. I cried for my grandmother, who lived with us, the one who always read to me when my parents were busy and who died six weeks after my father. I cried for the house we were forced to leave because it was accommodation with my father's job and the only home I had ever known, and for the other dog who was put down all those years before, not because she was ill but because she was considered too boisterous for our new home and because my mother would be working long hours to make ends meet. I cried for my great-aunt, the eccentric lady who had died when I was in my teens and who, apparently, I had resembled. I cried for my mother who had died when I was 25, suddenly and post-operatively before I could visit her. I cried for my aunt who had died when I was pregnant with my son, and who had, the nurses said, hung on as we travelled across country to see her, and who had died ten minutes after I arrived and was able to tell her I was there. I cried for them all and for so, so many more people I have loved in all the different places in my life. I wept for every loss, those remembered and those forgotten but still lodged somewhere in my soul. The tears, inseparable from each other, cascaded down my cheeks that day, each loss interwoven in a complex tapestry of grief.

Reflecting on the Bible account: David's story

How much grief can any one person stand? It is as though my whole life has a thread of the death of those I love running through it, and I am broken by sorrow. All of them are gone, and my heart is empty and aching with their loss.

Samuel was the first. I can still remember the day when he came to Bethlehem. I was content to watch my father's flocks, but then one day I found myself summoned, and to my astonishment Samuel anointed me, marking me out from my older brothers as chosen. From that day on he was there in the background of my life – I might not see him, but I knew he was there, a tangible reminder amid the madness of Saul's persecution that somehow God was in the middle of it all; that he would not abandon me or the promise I had been given that day.

I could not even mourn for Samuel with my countrymen, or be at his burial. Exiled as I was, hidden in Philistine territory, I could not honour my mentor as I would have wished, and I felt alone with my grief. My tears had to be hidden, private reminders of the loneliness of my separation from everything that was dear to me. Irrational as it was, I was angry that Samuel had abandoned me before his words, which had so altered the direction of my life, could come to fruition.

People think that if things have gone wrong in a relationship you don't grieve, but it's not true. In reality I think the grief is more complex. Oh, how I grieved for Saul – for what could have been, for the man he once was who I had loved and served. The later memories were there, of course, the jealous rage in his eyes, the whistling of the spear, those inner scars of the years I had spent fleeing him for fear of my life. But I remembered too how I had longed to soothe his anguish and sometimes, as I played my music and prayed, I had succeeded. And I recalled how we laughed when he dressed me in his over-sized army clothes before I fought Goliath, and the pride in his eyes as he promoted me. Yes, it went terribly wrong, but I had loved him like a father once, and he had cherished me as a son. And so I mourned him.

But it was not just Saul who died that day on Mount Gilboa. There was Jonathan too. Until what happened to Bathsheba's son and Absalom, I thought no pain could rip my heart out like his death. A friend who was closer than a brother, who had given up so much for me, whose loyalty to me was as great as to his father. I hated that circumstances and Saul's enmity had separated us for so long. Another death in that bloody battle.

War has claimed so much, destroyed so much, divided so many families. I miss Jonathan every day. I replay the conversations we did have and imagine the ones of which we were deprived.

Then Bathsheba's son. My poor, nameless son, who neither of us in our grief could dignify even with his own identity. A tiny scrap who represented to me my most terrible mistake, taking his mother from her rightful husband, exercising my power as king in a way that in time I so deeply regretted, despising myself. I wept for who he might have been, the son I could have had if I had sought God instead of succumbing to my acquisitive lust; shedding tears for his wasted life, for all that potential which would never be fulfilled. And I wept for Bathsheba, with her empty womb and empty arms, her breasts full of the milk she could never give him.

All those losses, and now this most recent, which eclipses them all. My son Absalom. There are always 'what ifs' in sorrow, but this time they were real, and mine alone. Why had I not forgiven him fully and received him as my son? Why had I been so cold? How hurt he must have felt, at home but not really accepted back? Why could I not have offered him the same mercy God had offered me? I was wrong, and it has cost me dearly. My indifference left him brooding, and as that turned to hatred, he plotted against me, trying to oust me as he had felt rejected by me. At first, I was angry at his rebellion, of course I was, but then as I looked within, I realised my own culpability. I saw how I had driven him away and I begged my officers to protect him somehow in the battle.

In my mind I replay how the news came. How my heart skipped a beat in fear when I saw the two men running towards me. My desperate question to the first – 'Is my son safe?' – and the way my heart was torn between hope and fear when he could not tell me. Then the second arrived, believing that he brought me good news of the defeat in battle when all I could think about was my son. I can still hear my cry of pain as I futilely roared his name over and over again as though that could somehow bring him back to me.

And in this greatest loss, I somehow grieve them all. My throat is aching with the wracking sobs and my eyes are sore. Yet somehow even this pain in my body is nothing to the searing of my soul. It is as if a limb has been ripped from me, and though I may somehow learn to walk again, I will never be the same. I can never now be whole.

(These parts of David's story are found in 1 Samuel 16, 1 Samuel 28:3, 1 Samuel 31, 2 Samuel 1, 2 Samuel 11, 12 and 2 Samuel 18.)

I have known a lot of loss in my life, of different kinds, and it has been my great privilege to walk with others who are grieving. The memories are fresh as I write. Holding a father, sobbing at the sudden death of his daughter, his body looking as broken as his soul. Sitting in a labour room with a couple, tears pouring down their cheeks as they held their stillborn son. Standing at the hospital bedside with two people saying goodbye to their beloved mother. The sound of earth trickling onto coffins at numerous gravesides, at times the rain mirroring tears from the mourners. On occasions like those there is nothing that you can do – only hope and pray that as you hold out your hands, or wrap your arms around those lost in grief, it is as though Jesus wraps his pierced hands around their broken hearts. Isaiah 61:1 includes the words 'He has sent me to bind up the broken-hearted', and the Hebrew word used is to 'wrap around'.

Not all loss is from death – even positive changes such as the birth of a baby, a new job or moving house involve loss (of sleep, independence, familiarity and so on). Other losses such as health, mobility, or reputation all bring their own kinds of grief. However, for most people, the sharpest and deepest grief they feel is when someone important to them dies. In society in general we respond in various ways to death. In the West, unlike other parts of the world, we often hide it away, seeing it as a failure of science and fearing to face our own mortality. Or we use platitudes to hide the reality – phrases like 'they are in a better place', or, if the person has faith, 'they are with the Lord'. I have known the latter used by the grieving person themselves as a way of minimising their loss, and my usual reply is, 'Yes, but they are not with you, and it is OK to grieve.'

Suffering a loss is, of course, hugely stressful, and so all the physical and emotional signs of stress may well be present, including sleep disturbance, loss of appetite and digestive discomfort. People will often site grief in their stomach or abdomen, even holding themselves there. The stages of grieving have been variously described,[3] the most commonly quoted including shock, denial, anger, bargaining, depression and acceptance. Our first response is often of shock, which may be experienced as physical shaking, weakness etc., especially if the death is unexpected, and is why great care should always be taken in breaking news that someone has died. Even if the person has been ill and the death was anticipated, relatives and friends can be taken off guard by still feeling shocked and need reassurance that those reactions are normal. It is not unusual to feel nothing at this stage – it is a kind of protective mechanism to shield us from the enormity of what is happening. This is linked with denial – sometimes literal and verbal: 'It can't be them, there must be a mistake.' This inability to face the loss will usually resolve in time, although occasionally it persists, shown for example by keeping the person's room as it was or laying their place at the table – both common in the early weeks but sometimes indicating a need for help if it persists beyond that. At this stage, if the person was not there when their friend or relative died, they often need details of what exactly happened as a way of making it real. There may not be many tears, and sometimes it is important to reassure the person that it does not reflect a lack of love.

Anger is often experienced during grieving and can be directed at various people, depending on the circumstances. In some cases there is a clear and obvious target, for example if someone has died as a result of the reckless driving of another. However, often there is not such a clear focus for anger. It may be felt, or even expressed, towards the medics who could not save the person who has died, despite their best efforts. The person who is grieving may blame themselves, saying, for example, that they should have called the doctor sooner. Sometimes the anger is directed at the person who has died, for not seeking medical attention for that particular symptom, taking the car out when tired, and so on. If we are seeking to walk with someone in their grief, we need to quietly accept expressions of anger and, as with all the stages, reassure the person that it is part of their grief. It is not unusual for people of deep faith to feel angry at God for not intervening to stop what happened. This is not the place for a debate on the theology of suffering – which is a task others can do far more ably than I can.[4] It is important, however, to allow that anger, whether in ourselves if we are the person grieving, or in the one we are trying to help. The Psalms are full of railing at God and I often point out to people that that raw expression of pain and anger are part of Jewish worship and can be of ours too.[5] I have found some of my closest times with God have been when I could express anger to him in a way I would not with anyone else, or sung freely and wordlessly with a lament which has come from deep inside.

Bargaining is the term used to describe our attempt to regain control, and is particularly a part of 'anticipatory grieving' – such as when we have been told a person is dying but it has not yet happened. People, even those with no clear faith, may bargain with God: 'If you stop them dying, I will believe/come back to church.' One of the most difficult aspects of death is that we cannot (usually) control it. We spend so much of our lives denying our ultimate helplessness by exercising control in all sorts of other areas to minimise our anxiety.

Depression is common in grieving – a kind of withdrawal inside, where there is little interest in the things we once enjoyed. This is not the same as a clinical depression needing medical intervention, though it can become so over time. The distinction is not easy to draw, but if the person can still function with ordinary tasks it may, again, simply be reassurance that is needed by explaining that this is natural and part of grieving. At times of emotional depletion, including grieving, we hunker down internally like a wounded animal seeking shelter. It is very important at such times not to allow the person to become too isolated, though this can be difficult. Part of the reason for withdrawal can be embarrassment on the part of the person grieving, because of the unpredictability of tears, so it can be really helpful to allow a safe space to cry. Sometimes other people, unsure how to be with someone who is grieving, may not persist in seeking them out. Those seeking to help can feel inadequate, and rather than risk saying or doing the wrong thing, simply avoid the person, which is actually much harder for them. One wise friend used to advise people to simply say 'I am so sorry for your loss' and then try to sense what the other person might find helpful.

The final stage is usually referred to as acceptance. This can be easily misunderstood – it does not mean there is no pain, but that we understand that the person has died and are making steps towards adjusting to this new phase in our lives. However, a significant loss will continue to impact us. I recognise that losing my father at an early age had, and still has, a profound effect on me. I'm acutely sensitive to loss, and have looked at times towards father figures, inevitably with a degree of disappointment. We are all unique, and our grieving, and the long-term implications for us, will be too.

Sometimes the stages of grieving are presented as linear – as though we move through them neatly and emerge the other side. I don't think this is a helpful way to think about it. It is all too easy to think we have come through a particular stage and then to be thrown when we revisit those feelings at a later stage. In reality, the order that we experience the different stages can vary, and we may return to one or more of them again. The stages are, I think, most valuable not as a tick box to expect to work through but in explaining to people that what they experience is normal. I have often, for example, found that people are worried because they have heard the person's voice, or a key in the lock, or even seen them, and are concerned about their own mental health. It is helpful to be able to say that this is because it is too much for us to take on the enormity of what has happened at once and so the brain recreates these experiences while it adjusts to the person no longer being there.

Personally, I have in some ways found J. William Worden's writing about the four tasks of mourning more helpful.[6] Like any task, we may start them and come back to them later. He described the first of these as accepting that the loss is real – to overcome the various forms of denial to come to recognise that the person really has died and will not come back and that reunion, at least in this current life, is impossible. This in itself takes varying amounts of time in individuals. It has to be reworked at times, even if only briefly when after a vivid dream of the person alive we wake up to find that the person really has died, which can be really distressing to experience.

The second task Worden describes is to allow ourselves to experience the pain of grief. In reality this may not be as automatic as it sounds. In the West, at least, we tend to hide from death and grief. There can be a tacit pressure to suppress feelings. I'm always distressed when I hear people say after a funeral 'Didn't they do well', when that usually means that the person did not show pain but were dry-eyed and appeared to have their emotions under control, which may be a relief to those who are not sure how to cope with it. I once conducted a funeral where most of the people attending had a number of severe additional needs. Their carers were concerned in case they shouted out or loudly verbally expressed their grief. I assured them that rather than this being disruptive, as they feared, it was more real and helpful than the stoical silence which is often there. A funeral should offer the opportunity to express our pain, or at least begin to. The subtle societal pressure to control our expressions of grief can feed into our own understandable reluctance to face its raw agony – for example, by distracting ourselves with busyness, or even making premature significant changes such as protracted travel or a house move. The spiritual clichés I mentioned earlier are another way of trying to avoid the pain. However, if we suppress our grief it does not go away and can take even longer to work through.

The third task Worden describes is to adjust to an environment where the person who has died is no longer present.

What that looks like will vary a great deal, depending on who the person was, their relationship to the person grieving, and the practical circumstances. To a young widow, for example, there will be adjusting to living alone, possibly raising children, perhaps managing finances and so on. Sometimes after a death we will need to learn new skills. When my father died, my mother had to return to nursing to support the family, which necessitated retraining as well as managing childcare issues differently, and also learning to deal with finances and a move from tied accommodation. Occasionally, this task of adaptation may entail adjusting to the element of release – such as when a surviving spouse has been nursing the person who has died. In that case their partner's death may be a bittersweet combination of a loss of both the person and the caring role, but also offer the opportunity to rediscover themselves again in other ways.

The final task Worden describes is the need to withdraw the emotional energy which belonged to the relationship with the person who died, and reinvest it into another relationship, of whatever kind. This can be quite difficult to imagine – with some people, especially in the loss of a long-term relationship, feeling it is disloyal to even contemplate. Yet loving another person does not mean we loved the person we lost any less. The thought of other relationships can also be frightening; I know for myself the early death of both my parents left me anxious when it appeared that other relationships might be lost – not just by death but also in other ways, such as a geographical move – and at times I felt I did not want to build new relationships only to lose them. Sometimes that emotional energy is invested not in a relationship with a person but in other ways, such as finding or re-finding a creative gift that has not had time or opportunity to flourish, or taking on new responsibilities in the workplace.

There are, of course, many instances when responses to grief will be different. At times relief overwhelms every other response – for example, if the person who died has been cruel or made life very difficult. If the person has been suffering a great deal, there can be relief for them but also for us, as it can be so painful to watch someone we love in pain or distress. It can be difficult to speak about this part of our reaction for fear of being misunderstood. Grief may also be delayed through circumstances, such as being overwhelmed by immediate practicalities. I did not grieve for my father for some years, for a number of reasons, including, as I said in the chapter on goodbyes, not being allowed to attend his funeral. I was later helped by someone who allowed me to talk about his death, write him a letter, and take some flowers to a local park. In many ways the grieving only began then.

The Bible is realistic about the reality of loss, and people grieving are found frequently in its pages – for example, Abraham for his wife Sarah,[7] Naomi for her two sons,[8] and the widow at Nain who has lost her only son.[9] Jesus himself wept at the tomb of his friend Lazarus, as we will look at later in Chapter 10.

One of the biblical stories of grieving I find most moving is the little-known story of Rizpah, told in 2 Samuel 21:10–14. She was the concubine (a kind of second wife but without the rights of the first) of King Saul, who had been killed in battle. When her two sons were killed to appease another tribe, along with five of Saul's grandsons, she stationed herself on the hillside where the bodies had been left. For five long months this extraordinary woman guarded the bodies and kept animals

and birds at bay. Deprived of the loving last act, to honour her
sons in burial, she was at least determined to make sure that
their bodies were not desecrated. In time, news of her actions
reached King David who, shamed into action, had both the
seven sets of bones from the hillside and those of Saul and
Jonathan buried properly. Her visible grief led to the proper
honouring of both her sons and several others.

This is a huge topic, with many resources available. This is
not a book on loss, but on tears, but I hope this chapter may at
least have been a useful overview. Grieving is a long road, and
we cannot hurry along it. We will never be the same when we
have lost someone close, and the first two years, at least, are
very tough. I love the way Jesus walked with the disciples on
the road to Emmaus,[10] allowing them to tell their story and
not rushing them. If you are grieving, be kind to yourself and
let the tears flow when they need to. If you are trying to help
others, walking with them for as long as they need is a costly
but wonderful gift to offer.

Some questions to reflect on

- List some of the different kinds of loss you have experienced, not just from death but in other ways.
- What is the impact of the losses you have experienced
  on the way you think, feel or behave?
- Are there any losses for you that are still quite raw? If
  so, what might help you as you continue to walk with
  your grief?
- Is there anyone you are currently helping through a
  loss? What might they need from you?

6

Tears of Distress

When Job's three friends, Eliphaz the Temanite, Bildad the Shuhite and Zophar the Naamathite, heard about all the troubles that had come upon him, they set out from their homes and met together by agreement to go and sympathise with him and comfort him. When they saw him from a distance, they could hardly recognise him; they began to weep aloud, and they tore their robes and sprinkled dust on their heads. Then they sat on the ground with him for seven days and seven nights. No one said a word to him, because they saw how great his suffering was.[1]

A current story of tears of distress

It was the first day of a new decade, and for once life seemed calm. The usual ups and downs of family life, but nothing that had prepared me for the coming storm.

My son invited me for a pint at the local pub. As we sat down, I smiled. 'This is a treat, son.' There was no smile in return, and my parent's instinct kicked in. Something was badly wrong. As I listened, I felt as though I had been kicked in the stomach. His marriage was over. My thoughts whirled around like dead grass in a desert squall and so I was immobilised, unable to find anything helpful to say. My pain for him as his father was mixed with so many emotions I could not name or distinguish, interwoven painfully with an emerging sense of guilt and a hundred questions. Why had I not realised? What kind of parent did that make me? What about his three children, so small? What would happen to them? And what about my daughter-in-law, who had been part of our family and who we had grown to love?

Over the next weeks and months, the sad story played out step by painful step, and we learned things about legally ending a marriage to which we had never wanted to be privy. The animosity that grew between them and the battles over the children left us all raw with sorrow. We tried to help as best we could, but our position one step removed meant often we had to watch helplessly, experiencing the deepest distress without being able to control or change anything. We ached for our grandchildren, caught in clashes not of their making, and at times felt frustrated with the adults involved who seemed unable to put their own needs aside to see the situation through the children's eyes.

This profound distress was not the only piece in my emotional jigsaw that year, however. As we wrestled with it all, trying to be available in the midst of our own busy lives, it became clear that something was wrong with my wife's sister. What we had thought to be distraction mixed with a little gently amusing eccentricity turned out to be early onset dementia, and a very aggressive form. We did all that we could, but it soon became clear that she would need some form of residential care before long. We knew there were some very difficult conversations and decisions ahead as we researched about lasting power of attorney and agonised with her in moments where she could glimpse what was happening and was so afraid. We were losing her by degrees. I tried to support her and my wife, but I was aware that my own emotional resources were beginning to run low.

I normally love my job as a social worker. However, that year it felt as though the privilege of helping others, being part of their story, had become a burden too heavy for me. It was not that anything had changed. Yet somehow the years of absorbing the pain of others had all combined, so that each time I was given a new client or heard about a setback of another, it overwhelmed me. I found myself wanting to do paperwork rather than see people – a sure sign that I was on the edge of burnout. My compassion was stretched and I wondered at times who I could turn to, who actually cared about me. Then two of my elderly clients died in quick succession. I stood dry-eyed through both their funerals, professional persona firmly in place, but slipped away as soon as I could to avoid the raw grief of those who loved them for fear it would unhinge me too.

In none of these situations, piling relentlessly upon each other, had I shed a tear. I felt somehow that I was the one who needed to hold it all together for everyone else. In all honesty, I think it was also my own fear that if I let go even a little, the whole edifice I had built around me to cope both with my own distress and that of others would crumble and that I would fragment entirely. I tried to explain to one friend, who in an attempt to be encouraging said, 'You will cope. You always do.' I understood they wanted to be reassuring, but I felt trapped in a role I had held since childhood: the one who manages amid all the turmoil, the serene one who could always handle whatever chaos might be around, or even inside, me. It felt as though no one could give space to my distress, and people wanted me to simply carry on, to keep up the role. Yet I was increasingly aware that the cracks were there. I was frantically covering them up as if disguise would render them safe, but time was running out. I was not superhuman, however much I or others wanted me to be.

The final straw came unexpectedly. A simple, routine blood test suggested strongly that I had cancer. Weeks later it was to prove not to be the case, but I did not know that at the time. Face to face with my mortality, it was not for myself I felt distress but for those around me who loved me, and those at work who depended on me. True to form, I sat calmly as the doctor spoke to me, even reassuring him that it would be fine, sensing his desire that I didn't break down, lest I disturb both his own composure and his cramped appointment schedule. My 'coping face' on, I made the follow-up appointment and left. Heading to a local park I found a secluded spot. Everything those months had held surfaced at long last, and I wept uncontrollably.

Reflecting on the Bible account: Eliphaz's story

I can still remember where I was when I heard about Job. I was grinding corn, my clothes covered in kernel dust. My wife had heard from the village women and rushed to find me. I sought out Bildad and Zophar at once. We were so deeply shocked. Such tragedy, so very close to home. Our friend. There was nothing to be done but to go and be with him. Our wives understood: sent us with their blessing for as long as we were needed. We had grown up together, the four of us, and were like brothers.

When we first saw him, we were distraught. Each one of us wept. He was barely recognisable. As is the custom of our people, we tore our robes as an outward sign of our inward distress. Stooping, I collected dust and sprinkled it on my head, needing some way to identify with my friend in his grief. We approached him in silence, our faces still wet with tears. He did not even raise his head, merely continuing to scratch rhythmically at the skin on his hands, its split and fragmented shreds somehow symbolising his broken spirit. For a time, a long time, we just sat there. Day turned to night, the inky darkness somehow bringing relief from the sight of this shattered man. For a week, as mourners we sat with him,[2] grieving both for all he had lost, but also for this friend in front of us who we seemed to have lost too.

I felt so helpless looking at Job. So many bad things in such a short time: his home, his family, his health. His distress was more than I could bear. I didn't have the right words to say to him, and I hated the feeling of impotence it gave me. I could sense that the others felt the same. And underneath it all, the twin thoughts of which we were ashamed – relief it was not us, and fear that it could be.

Then, after our week with him, he started to speak, his voice cracking at first from his protracted silence and the dry air of the desert where he had sought refuge. I was appalled by what I heard. Words of the deepest despair spewed from his mouth like blood from a gaping wound, somehow contaminating us all with its bitterness. There was no shred of hope, no acknowledgement of God except as some form of heavenly captor. I found it terrifying.

In my distress and yes, from fear lest everything I'd held onto might crumble, I felt I had to speak. Looking back, of course it is easy to see how wrong I was, but at that moment all I wanted to do was take refuge in my certainty, to cling to my inherited theology like a drowning man grabbing any wreckage, however flimsy. So I spoke up. God makes sure the innocent prosper, I told him, and punishes the guilty. That is how the world works. Inwardly I was thinking this must be so or I have nothing to hold onto. I stopped short of accusing him of wrongdoing, offending God, but only just.

For the first time he looked at me. I could not read his expression, but I was appalled at his response, protesting his innocence with no sign of apology to God. I was rendered silent for a time, and was glad when Bildad and Zophar took over. We had to make it right, you see, or so we felt. Even felt we had to defend God somehow. None of us wanted to face our own uncertainty and questions. Our beliefs must be unbending or they would break.

Job seemed as impervious to my friends' advice as mine, replaying the same message of despair and unwillingness to admit what he had done wrong. I tried again, more direct this time. Now words upon words of accusation spewed from me until I was spent.

I was stung by his reply, and his allegation that we were 'miserable comforters'.[3] We only wanted to fill the frightening void of both his misery and ours, to somehow try to give it meaning and a possibility of escape. My pain at my friend's distress and my inability to help was causing anger to rise in me, and finally it broke out as I hurled senseless accusations at him, laying every sin I could think of at his door in the hope that something would stick, that one of them would be the key to bring him to repent and save both him and us from this dark abyss.

He denied it all. I gave up then. I was not even sure who I was angry with any more. I just felt empty. The others continued, but I had nothing left to say.

And then the storm came. A strange desert storm but like no other I had seen. Lights flashed across the sky in a terrifying display of power and I was overawed, looking pointlessly for shelter. But not Job. He stood for the first time, weakly scrambling to his feet, upright with arms outstretched to the heavens as if listening. It was as if a peace came over him at last, and he stood there for a long time. Finally we heard, quietly from his lips. 'I did not understand'[4] – said in an accepting way, not the bitterness and desolation of before. And then, as the storm abated, he sank to his knees in prayer.

(Eliphaz's story is found in Job 2:11–13, 4, 5, 15, 22, 32:1 [by implication] and 42:7–9.)

It is easy, isn't it, to criticise Job's friends and think we could have done better. They did so well at first, weeping and sitting with him in silence. Until they spoke, they were, I think, profoundly helpful. I remember once a counselling supervisor encouraging me by saying how powerful a listening presence could be, but also warning me of the danger that was lurking as soon as we open our mouths to speak. I suspect all of us can remember occasions when our words were unhelpful, at least at the time, or when we have been on the receiving end of words that were inappropriate, or even damaging. When my mother died, I received a letter telling me that my mother had died because I needed to repent and come back to God. Looking back, I do think the writer was sincere rather than being deliberately cruel, but it was profoundly unhelpful to me as a young woman who by my mid-twenties had already lost both parents.

Some Christians, in my experience, can be far too skilled in judgementalism, and not always good at simply living with things that we do not understand. Certainty, and a set of clear theological explanations that cover every life situation, can appear to be appealing and reassuring, but as the book of Job shows us, we hold them too tightly at our peril. As the breathtakingly beautiful poetry at the end of Job reminds us, we were not there when God 'laid the earth's foundation'[5] and our understanding is limited at best.

When we try to accompany someone in distress, perhaps particularly when there are multiple causes for that distress, as with Job, it challenges us in a number of ways. The most obvious, of course, is that if we care for them, it causes us pain too, at a number of levels, as it clearly did for Job's friends. If we have experienced something similar, it can nudge sore places within us. If we have not, it can touch on fears, perhaps seldom acknowledged, that the same thing might happen to us. We might find it difficult to understand if it is something completely outside our experience. For those in the caring professions, including my own past and present roles of counsellor and minister, it can become exhausting, a kind of vicarious trauma. If we do not take care of ourselves[6] then compassion fatigue can set in and lead to an unhelpful rush to make things better, which can result in premature problem-solving responses which can be wounding rather than reparative.

The book of Job is a difficult one in many respects, but the themes are familiar. Job is wrestling with the contrast between the way he has thought about God previously and the God he sees as now unjustly afflicting him. It is part of the privilege of my job to often spend time with people who have become very unwell. For people of faith, questions frequently centre around wondering what they have done to deserve this, or how could God do this when they have faithfully worshipped and served him. They are thoughts I have heard frequently, and of course at times people abandon their faith, either for a time or even permanently, when disasters strike. It can equally be a stumbling block to those exploring faith, and though many books have been written addressing the problem of suffering,[7] it remains painfully problematic.

If we look to the book of Job for an intellectual answer to suffering, we will be disappointed. No explanation is given to Job, simply a beautiful description of the majesty of God, and the opening of the book poses more questions than it answers. The book is helpful, however, in giving voice to the way that many people feel in distress, as do other books in the Bible, such as the Psalms,[8] Jeremiah[9] and Habakkuk.[10] It also warns us against the traps we might fall into as we accompany others in difficulties, and gives a strong argument against the view that suffering and sin are linked in any simple way.

Above all, it reminds us that to sit and weep with those in distress might be the most healing thing of all.

Some questions to reflect on

- How easy do you find it to simply be with someone in distress, rather than trying to fix or explain their suffering?
- Can you remember a time when something unhelpful was said to you when you were distressed? What made it unhelpful?

- It was God coming close to Job and speaking to him that made all the difference, transforming both his suffering and his understanding of God. Can you recall times when you have experienced that in times of distress?
- Are you alongside anyone at the moment who is in distress? How might some of the lessons from the book of Job help you?

7

Tears of Fear

*They went to a place called Gethsemane, and Je-
sus said to his disciples, 'Sit here while I pray.' He
took Peter, James and John along with him, and
he began to be deeply distressed and troubled.
'My soul is overwhelmed with sorrow to the point
of death,' he said to them. 'Stay here and keep
watch.'*[1]

A current story of tears of fear

It was winter in the UK, though summer in Pakistan where I
had been for just over two weeks. What had started as a trip to
visit a friend from college, planned months before, had changed
completely from the original arrangements when a massive
earthquake hit the country. It caused widespread devastation,
the death of around eighty-seven thousand people with almost
as many injured, and resulted in nearly three million people
being made homeless and displaced. Our visit, instead of helping us to gain understanding of my friend's day-to-day life and
seeing his beautiful country, became a daily trip out from the
hospital base in northern Pakistan with provisions of rice, tea

and other basic foodstuffs. The evenings were spent bagging them into manageable-sized portions. On one occasion I had the privilege of giving blood to a heavily pregnant woman suffering complications who had made her way through the rubble to the safety of the complex.

For most of the trip I had felt nothing but distress for the people there. One day, making our way back from a scene of total destruction with the poignant sights of an occasional child's shoe or toy poking from the rubble, none of the team could speak. We simply sat in the van, some of us with tears rolling down our cheeks. There were no words.

The travelling had been complicated by the power of the earthquake, which had actually changed the topography of the area in some places. We frequently rounded a mountain pass to find that the road had disappeared or changed. On one occasion we had a rare afternoon off and our hosts intended to show us a lake nearby. However, when we got near the site, neither the lake nor the road was visible any longer.

The mountain roads in that area are normally hazardous, and often cited in lists of the world's most dangerous journeys. They are unpaved, little more than dirt paths, often only one vehicle wide and bending around blind corners. We were trying to reach some of the more remote areas, which meant we had no choice but to navigate these winding tracks up to higher regions. At each stop someone would have to jump out of the van to place blocks behind the wheels so that if there was any movement the van did not hurtle down the side of the mountain – there were still aftershocks occurring, and the loose dried tracks were insecure at the best of times, but now doubly so. On one outing, hearing the men speaking in hushed tones in Urdu, I asked them what they were talking about. Reluctantly they told me that some people had died in a landslide a few days before on that same route.

An additional difficulty was that in some regions white people were either viewed with suspicion, or at times kidnappings for financial gain had occurred. Although there was at that time more openness because of the huge scale of the disaster necessitating large groups of foreigners bringing medical and other aid, there were still risks in some parts. I can remember on one occasion carrying bags of food to a very remote camp in the dark and one of our party, only half in jest, asking how much the church would be willing to pay for us if we were snatched. On another we had to change our route because of a recent abduction.

Despite these dangers, it was not until we were near the end of the trip that fear took hold of me for the first time. I suppose it was cumulative, and perhaps sheer exhaustion was a factor. I will never really know. Up to that point at times I had been on high alert, yes, but with a manageable level of anxiety, mainly based not around safety but wanting to do a good job – the help we were bringing was a drop in an ocean of pain and need but still important to those to whom we brought it. I had not even been unduly perturbed when, sitting in the top floor of a small building, an aftershock had occurred. Looking at the faces around me I realised they were not unduly alarmed, and so I was not either. It is the same principle I always adopt when a boat is in choppy waters or a plane is experiencing turbulence – if the crew look calm or the stewards are still serving drinks, I don't get anxious.

On this particular day as we set off, I was not expecting anything different. It was only a day or two before we were due to fly back to the UK, and I was weary and looking forward to home comforts. About twenty minutes into the journey, I realised that these roads had some of the sharpest bends we had so far encountered. One side would hug the mountain, the other was a sheer drop. If there was an oncoming vehicle – which we could not see – then we would be in real difficulty. I trusted our driver and his local knowledge, but I felt a sense of unease rising. Then finally we stopped to visit a contact in a small village. Ahead I could see that the road branched in two. One, whilst much like the other roads, was a relatively mild route. The other clearly had the worst set of bends and drops we had seen so far. I had no idea which way we were going.

Citing the need for a toilet, I retreated to the small tented 'room' where I was out of sight. I was shaking, and for the first time I was truly afraid. Again the tears flowed, this time not in empathy for the suffering I had seen, but from sheer unadulterated fear, washing over me in a cold sweat like waves. Half as a prayer, half to myself I muttered, 'I can't do this any more.' I had never known fear like it – an acute dread, not for the distant future but for the immediate next few minutes.

In the event, I made a decision. If we were going right (the really sharp route) I would need to walk some of the way. I simply could not face another treacherous route. I could walk the most severe part down and catch them up at the bottom. I was done. I cried for a while, and then took a deep breath, wiped my face on my sleeve and headed back to the group.

'Which way are we going?' I asked.

'Left,' came the reply.

I got back in the van.

Reflecting on the Bible account: Peter's story

I'm afraid. We are all afraid. Most of all, my friend Jesus is afraid.

It all started at supper. This week has been so strange – the wonderful celebration as we rode into Jerusalem – I reckon that all of us were thinking, 'This is it – Jesus will declare himself Messiah, liberation from the Romans is coming and we are in the front row seats. Those three years away from our families have all been worth it.'

But then nothing happened. Well, something, but not what we expected: not teaching in the Temple that provoked the religious leaders but did not change anything else. He taught us privately as well, and I sensed both a growing sadness and an urgency in him as the week passed. On *yom hamishai*[2] he gathered us for a meal.[3] I just assumed this would be to discuss strategy. Time to tell us the plan, and our part in it.

From the beginning something seemed wrong, out of kilter. Because the meal was just us, there was no one to wash our feet. We all waited for someone else to do so, each of us reluctant to be the one to serve. Then Jesus took the towel and knelt at our feet. Well, I was having none of that. 'No, Jesus, that's not happening,' I protested. 'No choice, my friend,' he replied. 'Not if you want to be part of me.' 'All of me, then,' I said, but he just said that wasn't needed. Sometimes I struggle to understand him, I really do. It is like I get glimpses of what he means and then they slip away like the morning mist over Galilee. He spoke about washing each other's feet. Mm. I wasn't sure I was ready for that. Anyway, they look up to me as the leader. So, it would not be right for me to take the servant role. But now I remember Jesus, so lovingly wiping my callused feet and I'm not so certain.

Then there was Judas. He seemed so distracted. I wondered what it was all about, but before I could come up with a theory the evening took a darker turn. 'One of you is going to betray me',[4] Jesus said. I thought I had misheard. We had stuck with him all this time so we were hardly going to do that now, were we? Course not. I was about to say something when I saw a look exchanged between him and Judas. For a moment I thought I saw tears in both their eyes, but it must have been a trick of the light. Then Judas jumped up, as though he had forgotten something, and headed off, without a backward glance. Some errand, I supposed. I noticed as he got to the doorway, though, how dark it seemed outside. As though all the life had been sucked from the spring sky. It seemed eerily silent as he disappeared from sight.

Jesus said some tough stuff then, about us loving each other. Well, I do try, but some of them are so annoying. He kept talking about going somewhere. The only place he is going is to victory, I thought. Finally showing everyone who he is. So, of course, I said I would go anywhere with him, and was stung when he said I couldn't. Even more when he said I was going to be sifted like wheat but he was praying for me. Of course, being prayed for is great, but why single me out? And what did he mean? Surely we would be dancing that victory dance soon, and we would take our places beside him as he ruled?

When he said I was going to deny him, I was crushed. Devastated. Was that what he thought of me? He's the best friend I have ever had. I've left everything for him, followed him around the country, leaving my fishing business to others and missing my family like crazy. Of course I wouldn't deny him. Never. Unthinkable. Certainly not. Not me.

It put a sour taste in my mouth, when I had been looking forward to time together and finding out the next steps. Suddenly the food tasted like dust. I looked around at the others who looked unsure too. Where was this all leading?

Finally, he said we were heading out. Fresh air at last – I was getting stifled in this atmosphere of gloom and confusion. It would all be alright now, everything back to normal – whatever that was going to look like. So we headed to the garden. He'd always loved that spot. There are places, aren't there, that just draw you in? Feels like God is closer somehow.

Not that night. He told everyone to pray, and then took John, James and me a bit further away. Instructions for the inner circle, I thought. But no. He turned to us, and I had never seen him like that. He was wracked with pain; you could see it etched in every part of his face, as though he was in some private agony which was hidden from us. He told us to stay and watch with him and I thought 'I can do that. Of course I will do that. I have no idea what is going on but I won't let you down, Jesus.' I could tell the others were thinking the same. We watched him go just a few steps. I knew I should pray, but I wasn't sure what or how. I can do action, but seeing him there, his body hunched over, I felt so helpless. I closed my eyes to try to summon a prayer.

The next thing I knew he was shaking my shoulder. I'm ashamed to say I had fallen asleep. Three times that happened altogether. Every time I tried to stay awake, I really did. And I always managed it for a while. What really scared me was the little I did see before sleep overcame me again. Because I could see his fear too. I'd never seen that in him before. Joy, sorrow, anger even, but never fear. I'd always looked to him to hold us together and now – well, he looked as though he might fall apart. It was as though the weight of the world was on his shoulders, as though some horror was ahead that only he could see. Maybe the sleep was a kind of refuge because I could not bear to see him like that.

So now finally I've woken up, and as I look around, I can see torchlights snaking their way along the path towards us.

I'm afraid. We are all afraid. Most of all, my friend Jesus is afraid.

(This part of Peter's story, from the Garden of Gethsemane, is found in Matthew 26:36–56, Mark 14:32–52, Luke 22:40–53 and John 18:1–11.)

As I type this, I'm away for a couple of days' writing space. On the way here, at seventy miles an hour on the motorway, a car, its driver clearly distracted, pulled out just in front of us. Immediately I felt sensations you will all recognise from similar situations – my heart rate jumped, I felt sweaty, and was in a split second on high alert. I felt very real, if brief, fear.

Fear. Just the word can be unnerving, can't it? Yet fear is a universal emotion, which in the right circumstances can be life-saving. So, what is it, and when is it helpful or unhelpful?

Fear is a biological and emotional response to danger, and many psychologists[5] have suggested that it is one of only a very few innate, universal emotions.[6] It seems it is not unique to humans – that animals also experience fear when in danger.[7]

Interestingly, the biochemical response to fear is the same in every individual. In Chapter 11 I look at the topic of stress, and although there are differences between stress and fear,[8] the biology underlying it is the same, based on the 'flight or fight' system built into our bodies. When we experience a threat to our safety or survival (for some reason, descriptions of this mechanism often quote our ancestors encountering a bear), our bodies react in a way to make possible either fighting the threat or running from it. Specifically, the stimulus (seeing that bear) sends a message to the amygdala, an almond-shaped set of neurons deep within the brain, which then sends a message via the hypothalamus, the brain's 'command centre', to the adrenal glands, sited at the top of each kidney, to release adrenaline. This has various effects on the body: increasing heart rate and blood pressure, expanding the air passages in the lungs, enlarging the pupils in the eye, redistributing blood to the major muscles (so slowing non-essential things such as digestion) and maximising glucose levels, particularly in the brain. It also minimises the body's ability to feel pain. All these changes allow for action or for escape – in the example of a car pulling out, to react and brake quickly and safely to avoid a collision. With that ubiquitous bear, the alternatives would be to engage in hand-to-paw combat, or run for the hills. I know which I would choose. The third response, seen less frequently than flight or fight, is to freeze – we see this in animals who 'play dead' with a predator in the hope it then moves on. If fear is extreme enough, even in humans the result can be a kind of paralysis where the brain seems to stop working and we are unable to respond.

In contrast to the universal physical effects, the emotional response to fear varies enormously from individual to individual and in different situations, for several reasons. One is the assessment we make as to the reality of the threat, which will be variable. If we feel we have no control, such as in a situation of violence or war, then our fear will be greater, but there will still be a difference between individuals, depending on personality, training for those situations and so on.

Another factor is how we experience the adrenaline rush. Personally, I love theme park rides. One of my all-time favourites is Galactica (formerly known as Air) at Alton Towers, where you are face down, so as you loop the loops and skim close to the ground it really does feel as though you are flying. In that context, I love the adrenaline rush and am often the oldest in the queue. In fact, I've just stopped typing to watch a clip on YouTube, which is not as good as the real thing but was a delightful reminder. To some, a ride like that would tip over into terrifying. Our physical responses would be the same (I do briefly have all the physical results of the adrenaline), but whilst for me it would be pleasurable, for others it wouldn't be.

Some of our response to fear is based on experience. I was brought up in Cornwall, with a very healthy respect for the sea. On some days it can look calm and yet there are treacherous currents underneath which can sweep away the unwary. In addition, aged about 10, and before I could swim, I was thrown in the deep end of a swimming pool for a joke. I can still remember floundering under the water, swallowing it, and how terrified I felt. I still don't like water in my mouth at the dentist and have to fight quite hard to stay in the chair. This is despite the fact that I am never happier than when I am beside water, or on it – as long as it is in a decent-sized boat. Some years ago, I went with my family to a water park, and knowing my usual love of water, they thought I would be in my element. Not wishing to spoil the children's fun, I got in one of the large rubber rings and entered the assortment of flumes, filled with swiftly moving water which tossed the ring about, catapulting me upside down. I had to get off. I was absolutely terrified in the swirling water, much to the huge surprise of my family, who were, I'm glad to say, enjoying it hugely.

Whilst my feelings about water are strong, they do not amount to a phobia, which is an extreme or irrational fear of a specific object or situation. Some have some quite extraordinary names, such as triskaidekaphobia (fear of the number thirteen), omphalophobia (fear of the navel) or my personal favourite, anatidaephobia (fear that a duck is watching you. Honestly). Whilst sometimes a source of humour, of course the phobias themselves are deeply distressing to those who suffer them. There are cultural variations in the development of phobias; it is a sign of our era that nomophobia has been identified – fear of being without mobile phone coverage. Phobias can be very debilitating, particularly if the object or situation is one that is essential for day-to-day living, such as spectrophobia (the fear of mirrors) or the more familiar agoraphobia (fear of open spaces) which can keep someone housebound, or claustrophobia (fear of confined spaces) which can make lifts, flying, or events with crowds difficult or even impossible. The phobia can become more severe if we follow the natural instinct to avoid the object or situation we are afraid of. This reinforces the message to the brain that this is something to fear, and so the response becomes even stronger.

Phobias can be learned – for example if we have a parent who screams every time they see even the tiniest spider (the phobia being arachnophobia) – or the result of a particular trauma, for example where a person develops a phobia of blood following experience of an accident. It is easy to see the link with post-traumatic stress disorder (PTSD), an anxiety disorder resulting from trauma. However, where PTSD, a complex area outside the scope of this book, has a range of symptoms including nightmares, flashbacks and difficulty sleeping, a phobia is a very specific and focused response of fear which is only experienced when the object or situation, or pictures or representations of them, are present. Fortunately, there are a range of therapies which can help, many of which are based on unlearning the fear response.[9]

People of faith can be very conflicted about the experience of fear, feeling it betrays a lack of trust in God and is therefore sinful. However, I don't share that perspective. Where fear is the response to a legitimate danger, I believe it is a God-given protection for us, helping us to be vigilant, which should be honoured: something to be thankful for. Fear is an emotion, and as I will say in Chapter 10, about anger, I believe emotions are neutral – neither sinful nor godly but with the capacity to become either, depending on the behaviours which result. Far too many Christians already struggling with mental health issues have had their suffering increased by being told that they have a lack of faith or have invited demonic oppression. I believe God in his compassion comes alongside us to help, not to condemn. It is moving and poignant to think of the fear Jesus suffered in Gethsemane as he contemplated the cross, and it is a reminder that because he became 'God with us'[10] we are deeply understood in our most difficult moments, including frightening ones. The fear of the disciples at the time of Jesus' death is evident from their desertion and later hiding behind locked doors,[11] but they came through that time to share the joy of the resurrection.

The Bible in its realism does mention fear a great deal. The 'fear of the Lord' is a frequent theme, being variously described as the beginning of wisdom,[12] a fountain of life,[13] and a source of blessing.[14] However, this is usually interpreted as an attitude of awe and reverence rather than fear as we might think of it. It has also often been quipped that clearly the first thing angels are taught in angel training school is to open any conversation with humans with the words 'Do not be afraid',[15] or at least include them very early in the conversation. It would seem there is what we might call a 'holy fear' when God's presence is particularly felt, and which is quite different from the unpleasant and disturbing emotion we experience at other times. It carries an important warning that although we are to come freely as loved and forgiven children, we should avoid arrogant flippancy in our approach to God. There are a number of times in Scripture when we are encouraged to not be afraid (though not the often quoted 365 or 366, one for each day), linked with the positive encouragement to trust God. A number of the Bible characters clearly experienced fear. David writes in Psalm 56: 'When I am afraid, I put my trust in you'[16] – sometimes, it seems to me, we hold our fear in one hand, as it were, and our trust in the other, and both are equally valid truths.

The most often quoted verse on this topic is 1 John 4:18 – 'perfect love drives out fear'. Plucked out of context, it can be another Bible stick with which to beat the vulnerable. In context, however, it is linked to judgement – an assurance that through the love of God, we need not fear punishment when God wraps things up and puts them right.

The reality is that we will never be completely rid of fear this side of heaven. The tears of fear will inevitably fall, for ourselves or those we love. What we can, wonderfully, be assured of is that Jesus has travelled that road before us, and that ultimately 'neither death nor life, neither angels nor demons, neither the present nor the future, nor any powers, neither height nor depth, nor anything else in all creation, will be able to separate us from the love of God that is in Christ Jesus our Lord'.[17]

Some questions to reflect on

- Is there anything new that you have discovered about fear from reading this chapter?
- What were the things you were afraid of as a child? Which ones have remained, and which are no longer there?
- How do you react, both inside and towards others, when you are afraid?
- What might be some practical steps to help you when you experience fear?

8

Tears of Gratitude

> *As she stood behind him at his feet weeping,*
> *she began to wet his feet with her tears. Then*
> *she wiped them with her hair, kissed them and*
> *poured perfume on them.*[1]

A current story of tears of gratitude

It had been a long labour, over twenty-four hours, and with a number of complications, not least that the baby, my much-loved beautiful girl, had resolutely stayed the wrong way up throughout the end of the pregnancy. She was a breech delivery, which is now an automatic C-section but not at that time, and I had a registrar determined to avoid that. Midwives had come and gone, monitors had given them and us a fright at various points, and pain relief had not entirely been effective. I was more tired than I had ever been, and all I wanted was for her to be born safely. It was early morning, and I could just see the light filtering through the slatted blinds of the delivery suite. The night was ending.

And then, feet first, she finally emerged. She was blue – her head not yet delivered – and I felt fear as I had never felt it before, not realising, of course, that it was only because until she was fully delivered she could not breathe and turn that wonderful, relief-inducing pink. At that moment, as she for the first time fully came into the light and I saw her, the long months of waiting and the trauma of the delivery immediately dissolved away like mist with the rising sun.

Just then, a friend of mine who was a midwife in the same hospital and ending her shift, put her head round the door. Holding my precious girl as though I would never let her go, I called to her 'We've done it!' as the tears coursed down my cheeks, tears of gratitude to God for this precious gift who I knew would change my life beyond recognition.

Reflecting on the Bible account: the story of the serving girl at Simon's house

I saw her at once, of course. We women, we have radar for that kind of thing. The sort of woman we cross the street to avoid, and to stop our husband's eyes from wandering. The kind we don't know whether to despise, pity, or fear. Perhaps we don't want to think too hard, preferring to believe we would never make those choices, however bad things got, when in reality how can we be so sure what paths desperation would take us on, if our own lives had been different?

At first, she was just standing at the edge of the crowd in the courtyard. She would never have been allowed in his house, of course, him being a Pharisee, set apart from the rest of us in so many ways, but lots of people, even unlikely ones, often listened at the margins of his gatherings. My master, Simon, liked to host receptions for important visitors, rabbis who like this one had just preached at the synagogue. I never quite knew if his interest was genuine, or whether he collected celebrities like other people collect jewels. Somehow my uncertainty about that was especially true that day. He was a complex man, a peculiar mix of apparent godliness and yet sometimes, for all his law-keeping, there was a chill about him. Somehow his purity was cold and unattractive, excluding rather than drawing people in. Like greeting this guest. It isn't compulsory in our culture to kiss guests, to anoint their head with rose oil, or wash their dusty feet, but you would expect that for a visiting rabbi. Not that day, not for this man. But none of it was my business anyway. I'm just here to serve the food and be as invisible as possible.

So, at first the meal was continuing without incident. It was clearly special, as they were reclining and there were more spectators than usual gathered around. But I was not expecting anything out of the ordinary. Until the nudges started as 'that woman' was spotted by guests.

My attention drifting from the tedium of my task by watching their rather superior expressions, I saw with surprise that she was moving through the crowd. Some, realising who she was, parted like the Red Sea for fear of touching her and becoming unclean. She seemed not to care, weaving her way through them with a look of steely determination. It was only when she stopped by the guest of honour, the rabbi Jesus, that I realised what she was holding. An alabaster jar. For a moment I was really confused. What on earth could she be doing?

And then, as she stood behind him, I realised that she was weeping. Not just eyes moistened by emotion, but tears pouring, cascading down her cheeks and falling on to his feet. I was transfixed at this open display of emotion, unsure what to do next as the dinner party I was meant to be serving at came to a very abrupt halt.

More was to follow. Apparently completely unaware of our open-mouthed shock, she knelt at his feet. Out from the jar flowed the most beautiful perfume, its heady fragrance filling the air, the costly drops mingling with her tears as together they washed his feet. I dared not think how she had earned it. Or was it her dowry poured out on this stranger, the ending of all her hopes to marry?

Yet the greatest shock was still to come. As everyone gasped in horror, she let down her hair, flagrantly breaking every social rule in our society. I quietly put my hand up to check that my own was in place – it had only ever been let down in privacy with my husband, as to let it down elsewhere was grounds for divorce. It was as though somehow her shocking rule-breaking might be infectious.

She was oblivious, though, to our reaction, gently wiping both the perfume and her tears from his feet with her hair like a towel. And so, I looked more carefully, as the truth slowly dawned on me. It was not shame, or distress, as I had assumed, which had overflowed in such emotion. It was joyous *gratitude*. She was thanking this rabbi in the only way she knew. Her tears were a wordless hymn of loving appreciation.

As I tried to understand, I turned to glance at my master. How would he respond? What I saw unnerved me. His eyes were full of loathing, I sensed not just for this woman but also the rabbi who had inspired such an outpouring of love and thankfulness. After all, he had spent his life never mixing with people like that, so Jesus clearly couldn't be a man of God, could he? My master said nothing, but I could see Jesus looking, somehow not just at his face, but more deeply, as though he could hear every thought and was seeking a way to reach out to him too.

Then Jesus spoke. He told a story – about two people who owed a moneylender. Inwardly I shuddered. Debt in our culture destroys lives and families. One owed two months, one two years' worth of wages. Would it be prison or slavery next in the story, I wondered? But no, the debts were forgiven. Now I was laughing inside. No one does that. No one.

Jesus, though, was asking a question. Which of the two would love most the person who had freed them? Surreptitiously I watched my master. Grudgingly he answered, 'I don't know. I suppose the one who was excused from the bigger debt.'

Jesus looked at him, and I sensed a deep caring that sat alongside the challenge of his next words. He pointed out, I felt with sadness rather than offence, that my master had not offered any greeting, yet this woman had poured out her heart is such visible ways. My master found Jesus interesting: she loved him. 'Do you see this woman?'[2] Jesus asked. Well, they had all seen her, yet not one of them – me included – had *really* seen her. Not like I could tell Jesus had seen her. All the heartbreak, all the wrong turns, all the pain, all the wrongs she had done and the wrongs that had been done to her – he had seen it all, somehow enfolded it in his love, and let her find hope again. Because she has been forgiven, Jesus said, because she has crashed and burned and been restored, that is why she loves me so much, that is why she is so grateful. Her tears had washed his feet because his love has washed her heart. They thought she was making Jesus unclean, but he was making her clean instead. That is why her gratitude was literally pouring from her.

Now, as the dinner party dispersed, I was left wondering: where am I in the story? Like my master, Simon, I keep the rules, yet sometimes in my heart too there is a heaviness, a coldness, an ingratitude. Religion, turning up to worship, isn't enough. My socially acceptable sins need forgiving just as much as hers. Like that woman, I carry the cost of choices that have not been the best and I can see all the ways I am not like this incredible Jesus. Like her, I feel lost sometimes and am looking for love. I serve because I have to, to earn; she poured out everything in service to Jesus in gratitude because of all he had given her. Maybe Jesus can help me, too, find the love and freedom she had discovered? Then, knowing I am deeply loved, maybe I could pour out everything in thankfulness to him too. Maybe my life needs changing just as much as hers.

(The story of this anointing of Jesus is found in Luke 7:36–50.)

An 'attitude of gratitude' is always a phrase I have struggled with. I am not always a very thankful person. I'm more inclined to see a glass half-empty than a glass half-full. It is not deliberate – but rather an unwelcome result of that curious mix we all carry of personality and life experience.

If you Google the phrase 'attitude of gratitude' you get millions of suggestions; it is even possible to buy gratitude journals, and social media often challenges people to post on the subject, sometimes daily. This is, I suspect, in stark contrast to the actual prevailing attitudes in our society. The rise of celebrity and the images on social media showing people on holiday, smiling, or celebrating the achievements of their children feed a false impression that everybody else has more than we do, is having a better or easier time, and can lead us to focus on what we lack rather than what we have.

There are some things that gratitude is not. It is not, for example, obligation. If we receive a gift, and immediately are beset with guilt because we did not buy that person a present at Christmas, or for their birthday, that is not gratitude. In fact, it may hamper that relationship as we wrestle with a sense of indebtedness. Though genuine gratitude may result in action, anything which is given or done from that 'attitude of gratitude' – a gift, act of service etc. – needs to come from a place of freedom, not duty or compulsion.

Nor is gratitude born from a sense of deep inferiority – that we do not deserve anything, that we are worth nothing. Yes, grace, receiving what we do not deserve, is an important and profoundly biblical theme, but if we are too enmeshed with our sense of worthlessness, we will struggle to receive anything and therefore to be grateful. As a simple example, one of the things many of us wrestle with is receiving a compliment. For years I would bat them away, until I realised that doing so diminished the opinion and generosity of the person giving it. Nowadays I usually at least try to respond with a simple, 'Thank you.'

Gratitude also needs an appreciation of what we have received. 'It's the thought that counts' often means we are not, in fact, thankful for the specific item or deed. It is also related to the giver – we cannot be truly grateful if there is antipathy or active dislike for the person giving the gift or help to us.

The woman who anoints Jesus, who is one of my favourite Bible characters, exemplifies gratitude. She has received I believe, several gifts. Jesus makes clear in his riposte to Simon – 'her many sins have been forgiven – as her great love has shown'[3] – that she has already received forgiveness although frustratingly we do not know when or how. She is also about to be given another gift: restoration to a society which would have shunned her, through the accepting and indeed endorsing words of this well-respected if controversial rabbi. This surely would have given her a third gift, that of the repair of her undoubtedly shattered self-image. Meeting Jesus has not just enabled her to stand tall in privacy, but to crash the dinner party of the religious elite and, from abandoned love for him, flagrantly flout social etiquette to express her love and thankfulness by both her tears and her expensive ointment. In contrast, the implication is that Simon, the churlish host, does not believe he needs forgiveness and therefore expresses neither gratitude nor even welcome to Jesus.

This woman is not, of course, the only Bible character to express gratitude. King David, a man of immeasurable wealth, was able to trace the source of his riches to the God who creates everything:

> Yours, LORD, is the greatness and the power
> and the glory and the majesty and the splendour,
> for everything in heaven and earth is yours.
> Yours, LORD, is the kingdom;
> you are exalted as head over all.
> Wealth and honour come from you;
> you are the ruler of all things.
> In your hands are strength and power
> to exalt and give strength to all.
> Now, our God, we give you thanks,
> and praise your glorious name.[4]

Gratitude is always a response to something – we cannot be grateful if we have not received anything. Yet the Bible is clear that thankfulness should be something we do need to cultivate very deliberately. We can sense deep sadness in Jesus when ten lepers are healed and yet only one returns to thank him.[5] Though, perhaps surprisingly, not one of the classic virtues of medieval Christian tradition (wisdom, fortitude, temperance and justice were considered cardinal virtues and faith, hope and love theological virtues[6]), gratitude is clearly commended in Scripture in a number of ways.

The Psalms see thanksgiving as a starting place for worship. Psalm 100 bears the inscription 'For giving grateful praise' and includes the words 'Enter his gates with thanksgiving and his courts with praise'.[7] One minister I know sometimes asks the congregation if they are breathing, pointing out that in that case there is at least one thing to be grateful for. Gratitude is arguably central to worship, since our being able to come to God in prayer, song etc. is predicated on his gift to us of life, forgiveness and adoption into his family.[8] Thank offerings were part of the worship of the Hebrew community and this joining of thankfulness and sacrifice is an interesting one. At times in our lives worship may come from a deep place of pain and be very costly. At those times, worship with others can be important as the corporate thankfulness sustains us.[9]

Paul's letters exhort his recipients, and therefore us, to be thankful. He writes to the fledgling church at Thessalonica to 'Rejoice always, pray continually, give thanks in all circumstances; for this is God's will for you in Christ Jesus.'[10] We do need a word of warning here. This verse has often been misquoted as 'giving thanks *for* all circumstances' and teaching has at times been given that we should thank God *for* the bereavement, pain or difficulty, sometimes alongside the – at the very least unhelpful and arguably abusive – suggestion that God intends the suffering. As I recounted in the chapter about distress, when my mother died I received a letter saying God had sent (not allowed) this loss because I was not following him closely and so I should be thankful. In my early Christian life, I read several books (now mercifully missing from my shelves so I cannot cite them) which claimed that if the reader thanked God for their circumstances, God would use that to release the person from them. Such teaching seems to me profoundly unbiblical and potentially unkind. I cannot imagine that Paul who penned those words to the Thessalonian church, thanked God for his beatings and imprisonments. Indeed, clearly he desperately needed God's encouragement during difficult times.[11] What we can be grateful for is not the circumstances themselves but God's love, his presence with us, and the companionship and loving support of others.[12]

One final, and for me inspiring, story as this chapter closes. Some years ago, I had the privilege of pastorally supporting a couple whose baby had sadly died in utero. They had invited me to the hospital on the day of his birth, to be with them during that poignant and painful time. As the little boy's mother cradled her tiny son in her arms, the tears rolled down her cheeks in the most profound grief, yet she also through her pain prayed, thanking God for the time that they had had with him. I have rarely seen such deep faith: desperate pain and gratitude wedded together in the most exceptional way. It is a moment I will never forget.

Some questions to reflect on

- How easy do you find it to be grateful?
- Who or what are you grateful for in your life just now?
- How do you express your gratitude to others? And to God?
- Are there any difficult times that you can look back on and be thankful not for the circumstances but for anything that resulted from them?

9

Tears of Empathy

> *A large number of people followed him,*
> *including women who mourned and wailed for*
> *him . . . It was now about noon, and darkness*
> *came over the whole land until three in the*
> *afternoon, for the sun stopped shining. And the*
> *curtain of the temple was torn in two. Jesus*
> *called out with a loud voice, 'Father, into your*
> *hands I commit my spirit.' When he had said*
> *this, he breathed his last. The centurion, seeing*
> *what had happened, praised God and said,*
> *'Surely this was a righteous man.' When all the*
> *people who had gathered to witness this sight saw*
> *what took place, they beat their breasts and went*
> *away. But all those who knew him, including*
> *the women who had followed him from Galilee,*
> *stood at a distance, watching these things.*[1]

A current story of tears of empathy

I was sitting with Nizar and Maya,[2] as I had many times before, in the church flat where they had lived for the last three years.

They had come to the UK as refugees from Syria with their 14-year-old daughter, but their two sons had been unable to come with them. One because he was not a minor and so didn't qualify for resettlement with his family, the other because as a teenager he had been detained in a Syrian jail for refusing to fight in the war, and was still there when his sister and parents were brought to the UK. Now the brothers were in Turkey and I was at the flat to talk to Nizar and Maya about how we might go about reuniting them.

We needed to talk about the experiences of their sons; the suffering and circumstances that might demonstrate vulnerabilities that could help their chances of resettlement. I knew most of their story already, I'd heard it in bits over the last three years, but this day, hearing it so unfiltered and with such desperation from the lips of their dad, I experienced the story in a whole new way.

It seems so inadequate to summarise their pain in words on a page. Even the most graphic description doesn't pack the punch I felt that afternoon. But we spoke for around ten to fifteen minutes about their separation from their family and the physical and mental torture one of them was forced to endure while in jail.

The truth is that when I shed that tear, it wasn't for them. I was, of course, desperately concerned for their wellbeing and couldn't imagine the agony they had endured and continued to face – but I'd never met them. Their mother, on the other hand, was less than 6 feet away from me and looked paralysed with fear and helplessness. My tear was for her.

I've noticed since becoming a dad that every TV show, movie and news story that portrays the suffering of a child affects me so much more than it once did. It doesn't matter how far removed the circumstances of the distress are from my experience, or those of my children – it just somehow evokes the universal, unremitting pounding that parental love so often has to endure. The truth is that my kids haven't suffered anything like the trauma of these young men and I haven't had to witness it from a distance in the way Nizar and Maya have been forced to. Yet I'd never felt empathy as strongly as I did then. In that moment I think I truly shared their pain – not nearly as brutally, not nearly as relentlessly, but it was so much more than sadness for them, it was sorrow *with* them.

I didn't sob. It was, at most, one solitary tear that barely made it to the end of my cheek before it dried up or I wiped it away – I can't remember which. But Maya saw it and I saw her shoulders slump, her fists relax and the slightest smile momentarily surface. I didn't ask Nizar to translate whatever she said next (Maya barely speaks any English) – I knew what she was trying to communicate. 'Now I know you understand – now I trust you – don't let me down.'

Reflecting on the Bible account: the story of a woman from Galilee at the cross

We had followed him this far, and were not going to turn back now. We had been there from the beginning, supplying food when he needed it; funds too, sometimes. Part of me wanted just to go home: not from fear for myself but for him, my head echoing with the senseless baying of the crowd who less than a week ago had welcomed him as King. Such a confusing shift in the atmosphere of this, our finest city, from the vibrancy and celebration to this coldness, fury almost, as though his very goodness had filled them with a violent rage. I was not sure

I had the strength to stay or had anything within me which could help. Yet I could not desert him now.

And so first of all we stood at the side of the track up to Skull Hill, huddled together though we knew nothing could bring us comfort. Then we saw him, and at that very instant my hope for any reprieve was shattered. He was marked from the whips, tears of blood coursing down his cheeks from the crown of thorns which had been ruthlessly forced on to him, mocking his true identity. But more than that, it was as if he carried not just that crossbeam, a heartbreaking reminder of his destination, but the weight of everything, the very universe, the world's past and present somehow telescoped in that one moment of suffering. I shook off the thought, but still, as I caught his eyes scanning the crowd – not with anger or judgement but with love – something within me broke. The tears came, and with them heaving sobs, for this man and his suffering, for the life which he had lived caring only for others and for us which was now being wrenched from him in the most humiliating of ways. For the injustice of it all. For the loneliness I sensed in him – where were those men, content to follow him when the miracles came, but apparently now abandoning him at the last?

We reached the place at last, jostled by the crowd, herded by the soldiers like animals heading for slaughter. But it was only his death, not ours, and it was for him that I continued to weep. This gentle man, who had been so moved at Nain and at Jairus's house, who had wept at the tomb of his friend Lazarus,[3] now rendered helpless in the face of his own terrible end, pain of every kind etched in his face and most supremely evident in his eyes. No tears from him, just that gaze which took us all in, somehow even then holding us in an embrace of love and – at the moment when it was most needed and least deserved – forgiveness.

We had to hold Mary up as they nailed him, and the rest of us turned our faces away, hearing his shout of agony but also those words of release for those who were doing it: 'they do not know what they are doing.'[4] Don't they? I could not understand everything that was happening here, as if forces were gathered which I could not see, and as that eerie darkness descended it seemed evil conspired to blot out his light and life even more than any hostile crowd, uncomprehending religious leaders, or corrupt empire could. Still my tears fell, and in the end I stopped trying to wipe them away and just let them flow. I might not understand, but still I could weep for him, Mary's boy and our greatest friend.

(This part of the story is found in Matthew 27:32–56, Mark 15:21–41 and Luke 23:26–49.)

Some years ago, acutely distressed about a situation very close to me over which I had no control, I was sitting opposite a friend attempting to explain. Although someone who talks for a living (among other things), actually when I am talking about deep and personal things I can find it difficult, using a lot of words, a kind of verbal haemorrhage, yet being unable to express the actual feeling, or know that the other person understands. Sensing my difficulty, my friend came and sat on the arm of my chair, putting both arms around me so that I was held in their circle, rather than simply putting one arm around my shoulder. Although no words were used at this point (they used many helpful ones later), it was actually a profoundly empathic response. I felt as though everything in both my internal and external world was shifting, splintering, and I had no idea how I was going to hold myself together, never mind anyone else. This encircling somehow communicated a deep understanding of what I had been unable to voice. Physical contact is not always the most empathic response – indeed at times it might be interpreted as trying to stop the distress because of the listener's inability to deal with it – but on this occasion it was exactly right.

Empathy is one of the key concepts in counselling. Carl Rogers, the originator of person-centered therapy, saw it as one of the three core conditions for effective therapy.[5] However, it is, in my opinion, one of those qualities which is actually quite difficult to define, although we instinctively know when we have experienced it from another person, as I did that day. Equally, we know when we have not, which can be at best jarring and at worst positively hurtful. Empathy is finding a way to see the situation from the perspective of the other person, which is a great deal harder than we might think. My experience in working with counsellors, pastors and students over many years is that undoubtedly some people are more naturally empathic than others, and although some skills can be taught or honed, there will always be a variance in the degree to which people can respond empathically. Sometimes we can sense that and know not to reveal our true feelings or struggles to a particular person. On other occasions we get 'burnt' by an unhelpful response and learn not to open ourselves to that person again. Certainly, I have a very short list of people I will be truly honest with, though I recognise we are all different in that regard and some of us are more open than others.

The word 'empathy' originated with the Greek word *empatheia*, meaning affection or passion, but gained in use following the translation into English of the German word *einfühlung* (literally 'feeling into') by the psychologist Edward Titchener in 1909. It may be easier to begin by saying what empathy is not. It is not the same as sympathy, where we are caught up in having the same emotional response. Over the years in training others in listening, I have used the image of passing someone who has fallen in a river and is drowning. Empathy is keeping one leg on the bank and reaching out a hand: sympathy is jumping in, risking both of you drowning in the emotion. Often if people have had a similar experience (for example, a loss), it is sympathy they feel, and they are more inclined to draw, sometimes unhelpfully, on their own experiences rather than put themselves in the shoes of the other. There are at least two unhelpful ways to impose rather than use our own history. The first is to say to someone in distress, 'I know just how you feel.' We might know how we felt in a similar situation, but (at the risk of stating the obvious) we are not them and no two situations are identical. The other danger is that we move into recounting our own experiences, particularly if they are not completely resolved. Following a very difficult delivery of my first child, I was amazed how many women, hearing it was complex, told me their own stories in great detail. Whilst I hope it helped them, actually what it did was take away my opportunity to talk through what had happened. It was several years later that a man, with no direct experience to share, listened with great empathy and allowed me to be at peace with the memories.

Empathy is also distinct from pity, which can imply a helplessness on the part of the person suffering and has the potential to be experienced as patronising. It is also not necessary to like someone or approve of their behaviour to experience empathy. When I was counselling I did not always immediately warm to the clients I saw – in reality, at first meeting, my feelings varied.

However, I discovered that as I heard their stories, and worked hard with both mind and imagination at putting myself into their world, I was able to find empathy and compassion, and hopefully to express it.

To experience empathy, it is therefore hugely important to understand another person: what they think and feel, their values and internal world. This is achieved by careful listening to their story, and using our instincts and our life experience (without making assumptions or imposing our experience onto them) to inform us. It is also crucial to be able to communicate that understanding to them. We may genuinely be empathic, but if we do not demonstrate that in our words or actions, it will not benefit the other person. When we can, it is enormously powerful and potentially healing.

In the Bible story above, the woman demonstrates her empathy by a combination of her tears and her presence. There is nothing she can do for Jesus in his final hours, though it is clear that previously the women from Galilee have supported him in his ministry, including in practical ways.[6] It is impossible for us to fully understand the horror of the cross, for a multitude of reasons, including both its unique nature and our cultural and historical distance. In attempting to do so, some have concentrated on the physical elements, which were clearly shocking and appalling.[7] However, my own sense is that the emotional and spiritual aspects were in many ways far more distressing. We catch, for example, the sense of forsakenness expressed in Jesus' words quoted from Psalm 22: 'My God, my God, why have you forsaken me?'[8] We have no record of the male disciples being present aside from John,[9] but the women, in remaining there to the end, are able to reach out emotionally to Jesus, to silently communicate that he is not alone despite the emotional toll the experience must have had on them.

It is clear that Jesus himself was a deeply empathic person, which is undoubtedly one of the many reasons people were so drawn to him. In the next chapter we will look at Jesus' tears at the tomb of his friend Lazarus. Roy Millar expresses it like this: 'Jesus' empathy with Lazarus and his sisters may have been intensified by His awareness of His own impending suffering and death, and the resulting grief that this would inflict on His own family of faith'.[10] Empathy is therefore an essential quality to develop if we seek to be like Jesus, and at times I think it can be a gift of the Spirit. While writing this, a friend shared a story with me. She had been visiting another friend's parents' church up in a mountain in the Philippines. Just two weeks before the church had suffered a bereavement, when a 19-year-old boy suddenly dropped dead without warning. As my friend sat in the service, a woman caught her eye – each time they looked at each other my friend started crying. She sensed her pain and somehow knew she was the boy's mother. Afterwards, they had a beautiful time simply holding each other and crying, and she was able to minister to this heartbroken mother with the words she felt God gave her.

This brings us back to the link between empathy and shared experiences. As I indicated earlier, if the situation the person is describing is familiar from our own lives, it can be unhelpful if this is imposed upon or supersedes listening to the other person. However, where it is carefully used internally by the listener and then communicated in a tentative way, it can be a source of valuable insight. Sometimes it can be helpful to ask gently, 'I wonder if you feel/felt . . .' without needing to say that we have felt the same thing, or why, and moving on if that was not what the person we are listening to has experienced. In the story above I believe it was a mix of my friend's own experience of bereavement, her natural empathy and compassion, and a work of the Spirit which combined to bring what I am sure was a healing experience for this traumatised Filipino woman without her ever putting her own experiences into words.

Thomas Keating tells a story[11] which sums up well the topic of this chapter. He recounts a meeting of leaders from different world religions where Archbishop Dom Helder was invited to speak about the situation of the poor in Brazil, as he had been involved with what are called 'base communities'.[12] As he started to speak, he began also to weep, and continued for several minutes. The group waited for him to continue, to say what he had planned, but he was unable to. As Keating summarises it: 'The memory of the destitute and the realisation of their desperate plight left him with just one response: tears. Nothing has ever so convinced me of what it means to be destitute as his face at that moment.'[13] He had witnessed, and been impacted by, tears of empathy.

Some questions to reflect on

- Think about an occasion when you experienced empathy from another person. What made it helpful?
- Think about another occasion when the response someone made was not so helpful. What made it less so? How can you use this to help you in your own listening to others?
- How good are you at being empathic? It can be hard for us to judge for ourselves – so why not ask people you trust to give you some honest feedback?
- How can you continue to grow in being empathic? What steps can you take?

10

Tears of Anger

Jesus wept.[1]

A current story of tears of anger

I shall never forget that Palm Sunday. It was the day God opened my heart to a truth that had, until then, really only been in my head. It was going to be a very good year, at least that was my dream. It was the year I had decided to retire and give myself plenty of time to plan for those days when after forty-six years of non-stop paid employment I would at last be my own boss, with time and resources to enjoy the rewards of my labour.

It was also going to be a very good year as my wife and I planned to go on pilgrimage to the Holy Land with a group of Christians from local churches. Meetings were held, briefings given and the date and times set for the 'trip of a lifetime'. Packed and ready, the day finally came for the not too early departure from London Heathrow. Then the telephone rang. I recognised the voice immediately and thought how kind it was of them to ring to wish me a happy holiday. But no, the call was for a very different reason and one which would change my life for ever.

Just a few days earlier we had visited my older brother and his wife and learned he was to have a simple procedure to remove a polyp from his stomach, all done through keyhole surgery, meaning recovery would be swift. Good news, indeed, as his wife was suffering from dementia and would find it difficult to cope on her own even for a few days. The telephone call was to tell me my brother had died in hospital. The simple procedure had turned into major surgery from which he never recovered. As a result, there would be an inquest and this would delay the funeral – the caller said we should still go on the trip; after all, it was what my brother would have wanted.

I was very angry: angry with the specialist who had intimated the routine nature of the procedure, angry with the surgeon who had removed his stomach, but above all, angry with God.

I don't remember travelling to the airport. I have a recollection of being asked by an El Al security person if I was carrying a gun. I remember most of all sitting on the aircraft seething at God. I started to keep notes of my feelings. How do I feel about this? What have I got to say to God, who seems adept at ignoring my prayers? What does it do for my own fear of death? If you had been there, God, my brother would not have died.

> Where were you, God? Are you as
> Real as that call, that death?
> Or are you just a wish, a hope,
> A dream, as fickle as fog which
> Blows away, or burnt up by
> The sun a million miles away.

I needed something to ease my anger and the hymn 'O Worship the Lord in the Beauty of Holiness' started the healing process with the words:

> Comfort your sorrows, and answer your prayerfulness
> Guiding your steps as may best for you be.[2]

Then God showed me this verse from Psalm 116: 'Precious in the sight of the LORD is the death of his faithful servants.'[3]

My brother had certainly been faithful all his life. He and I had sung in the church choir, he had been a deacon and in these latter years, whilst his wife was helping in Parent and Tots on a Monday morning, he had cleaned and tidied the church. He could be relied upon to be there at every funeral service; how ironic that now he would be in that same church for his own. My anger remained. Surely if God had been there in that hospital, my brother would not have died?

Palm Sunday in Jerusalem meant Eucharist in St George's Cathedral. I was not in a good place, not helped by people in our party insisting on looking in the shops along the Via Dolorosa and making us late for the service. Compensation came when we were ushered to the front and served communion by the Bishop of Jerusalem.

Having visited so many churches and basilicas from the Church of the Nativity to the Church of the Holy Sepulchre I was frankly 'churched-out' and the final straw came when we were due to visit the Church of Lazarus in Bethany. I refused to go in. I knew all this Bible stuff. I had been going to church ever since I could remember and did not need another building to add to my list. My wife can be very insightful sometimes and said she truly felt I needed to enter this church and, furthermore, to stop making a scene.

With my anger in check, in I went and there above the altar were the words in Latin, '*Ego sum resurrect et vita*'. Even I could understand what the words meant. 'I am the resurrection and the life.'[4]

The dam burst, my tears flowed freely and that Palm Sunday changed my life forever. I wrote, continuing the poem quoted earlier:

Jesus on this day
Rode triumphant to his death
That I might see and live.
This Jesus blows in faith
And fickle fog is finished
Mist and night defeated
By cross and resurrection.

From head the truth had travelled to heart. This was a vital step of faith for me because in the next twelve months I experienced four funerals and a wedding. The story of those tears and the truth I learned stayed vivid for me through that year and does, still, to this day.

Reflecting on the Bible account: Martha's story

It was all too late, and I was angry. Sad, yes, and so heartbroken, but underneath that desolation sat a rage born of my disappointment. Why hadn't Jesus come? We had sent word that Lazarus was sick, and he had healed so many. We never doubted that he would come, or that he would heal Lazarus. He was his friend, his good friend. He loved him. He had told him that. He had showed him that. But what use was that love when we needed him and he stayed away?

While Lazarus was sick, we had hope. We kept scanning the horizon, looking for Jesus' familiar gait, accompanied by his other friends, eager to reach us, to help. But all we saw was the scrub bush, and the sun, setting, rising and then setting again.

And then Lazarus died. Yet still we took courage. 'Remember Nain,'[5] my sister said to me, 'and Jairus's daughter.'[6] We almost delayed the burial to wait for Jesus but we knew in our hearts we could not do that, and the village was already gathered in support. So, we wrapped our precious brother, our tears soaking the cloths. For one last moment before we covered his face, I touched his cheek, hardly able to believe that I would never see him again. Then finally the stone was rolled into place, and a rock settled in my heart too. I busied myself with the arrangements, my tumbling thoughts invaded by the memory of Jesus' gentle rebuke those months ago that I was 'worried and upset about many things'.[7] Well, what do you expect now, Jesus? Of course I am harried, preparing a funeral gathering I never wanted and which you could have prevented. Where is that love you spoke of for us now, Jesus? I'm alone in the dark and still you have not come. Are you playing some kind of game with me, with us all?

So, our month of mourning began. The dust was thrown, the robes ripped, the mourners leading the wailing, the noise searing the rawness of my grief rather than bringing comfort. I nursed my anger to me, a way to hold the pain at bay. The whole village was there and I thought I heard them whispering in corners about our friendship with Jesus and how he had let us down. Or perhaps that was just my thoughts, echoing emptily round the house which had once rung with my brother's laughter.

Just then, as I thought the storm inside me must surely erupt, he came. My friend had run quickly to tell me that she had seen him outside the village, heading towards us. At first I was not going to meet him, to express my fury by silent absence. But I decided to go, my steps propelled by the inner rage. I stood in front of him, meeting his eyes but not waiting to see what they held for me.

Through gritted teeth I spat out: 'Master, if you'd been here, my brother wouldn't have died.'[8]

Then I paused. That was not how I was meant to speak to Jesus. From within I wrenched what was left of my respect and retrieved what I imagined I was supposed to say. 'Even now, I know that whatever you ask God he will give you.'[9]

'Your brother will rise again.'[10] Jesus' apparent calmness somehow failed to pacify me. I was exasperated. I knew the teaching. I'd heard people recite Daniel 12 and those beautiful prophecies from Isaiah.[11] Yes, resurrection would come, but what use was that now? Would that put food on the table for Mary and me? Would that ease our pain or fill our empty hearts?

Then I looked – really gazed at him. There were so many emotions in his eyes, each one vying with the others for supremacy. I saw sadness, yes, somehow much deeper than my own, as though the weight of the world was there. I could see, too, that he understood me, accepted my wounded anger and somehow enfolded it in the love that I had so recently doubted. Yet at that moment what I saw with the greatest clarity was his authority. A power that went even beyond the miracles that we had heard about from garrulous Peter over supper as we provided Jesus a much-needed oasis. He spoke then, with a voice that somehow rang across the years, beyond my small corner of Palestine to a wider time and place I could not see, huge words, shocking words, words I could not fully understand then, or perhaps even now. 'I am the resurrection and the life. The one who believes in me will live, even though they die; and whoever lives by believing in me will never die. Do you believe this?'[12]

From within my broken spirit hope and trust gently began to be born again, and hesitantly found words. We had thought he was the Messiah, the Christ. Could I hang on to that now, even amid disaster? I gave voice to my faltering faith. 'Yes, Lord, I believe that you are the Messiah, the Son of God, who is to come into the world.'[13]

Suddenly, I knew I needed Mary with me. We had our moments, sisters that we are, but I wanted her at my side. Besides which, Jesus was asking for her. She rushed to meet him, finding him still outside the village. Unlike me, she fell at his feet, where she so often was when Jesus was with us. Like me she expressed her disappointment, even using the same words, but unlike me she spoke them somehow from a place of adoration, even worship. Where I had defiantly stood my ground, she knelt weeping at his feet. As I watched her, my compassion mixed with envy, a sound rose from his throat, almost like a lion's roar. I could see anger was there in him too, a deep distress at our suffering, at death, at everything that was not as God intended and which broke his heart as well as ours.

As one, Mary and I spoke together. 'Come and see, Lord.'[14,15] Yes, I thought, still not quite ready to let my anger go, come and see. Come and see the grave. Come and see the wailing. Come and see the rock which seals away our precious brother from us. Come and see how our hopes are dashed and our future uncertain. Come and see how death has ravaged our home and destroyed our lives. Come and see.

And then he wept. Not a loud, contrived wail like the professional mourners, but silent tears coursing down his cheeks, winding their way through the dust which the day and the journey had left on his face, just as we had wound our way in sad procession from the village to the graveyard. I saw my own broken heart echoed in his, reflected in that silent mirror glistening on his cheeks. Jesus wept.[16]

So, we took him to the tomb. Again, I saw his anger, the deepest distress, but almost before I could register that, his next request shook me to the core. A demand which if it had not been so ridiculous would have almost been amusing. He asked me to arrange for the stone to be removed. Now I was incredulous. Why would he want that? Did he want to say his final goodbye, to lovingly touch his friend's cheek in farewell as I had? It was too late. That opportunity had been lost with the delay that he had inexplicably chosen. 'He would stink, Lord,' I said, a tacit reminder of how long Jesus had delayed. What point now, when his spirit had left and his body was just a shell?[17] But in the end, what option was there? So we ordered the men to remove the stone, their faces expressing dismay as well as exertion, but not feeling they could go against our wishes. He prayed, and then shouted as if Lazarus would hear him 'Lazarus, come out!'[18] Such power and authority, like nothing I had ever experienced. We all stood, open-mouthed. Later I was to smile, thinking how he must have named him to stop the whole graveyard coming to life.

I didn't expect anything, but somehow still held my breath. And then, as my tears of anger and sadness stopped and then dried in the heat of the day, out from the darkness he came, hesitant and shuffling as limbs returned to life and my every 'if only' faded away like morning mist with sunrise. Tears flowed again, fresh tears, tears of joy, of relief, tears of reunion as we gently removed the coverings we had only put there four days before, tears as we held him, tears as we explained to him that Jesus had come after all. Tears, above all, as we took him home again.

(This part of Martha's story comes from John 11:1–44.)

In my experience, the Christian community is often not very good at dealing with anger. Despite the teaching of Scripture that we can be angry but not sin,[19] many church people seem to believe that all anger is wrong. At the very least, many make a distinction between righteous and unrighteous anger, the former being permissible and the latter not, a difference that in reality I suspect is not always easy to make. I once had a member of the congregation I was serving say to me that she had assumed I never felt anger because I am a minister. I barely knew where to start in answering her.

When I run training sessions on dealing with our anger, I often ask the group what words they associate with it. In most groups, the vast majority of responses are ones we might consider negative – rage, violence and so on, rather than alternatives such as justice, empowerment or energising. It is an emotion that many of us do try, with varying levels of success, to stifle.

Yet anger is one of the first emotions we experience, and is part of our survival system. If you watch a baby who is hungry when there has been a delay in feeding them, you can see that what begins as distress moves on to fury and there is a discernible difference between the two. This observation helps us to understand at least one of the sources of anger: it can be a response to a need which is unmet, or to pain. When I was counselling, I often used to ask clients if, should they stub their toe, they were more likely to cry or swear. Some Christians were horrified I could even ask that as a question, but I know several godly people who are honest enough to admit that they can tell when their stress, distress or anger levels are rising by their language, even if it is thought rather than said. Some of us in pain will respond with tears, others with anger, the reality being that anger is frequently the flip side to pain. Martha's apparent anger springs from what is arguably the deepest distress we ever face, the loss of someone she loves, in her case, her brother.

Martha also shows us another side to anger. Our anger is fuelled when we feel helpless – again think of that hungry baby – and death is something over which we have no control. The sisters have done what they could in sending for Jesus, but they cannot control him and he does not come. They are helpless to stem the disease racing through their brother's body, and unable to summon the only help available to them. They are left to impotently watch their brother die. It is a helplessness many of us have gone through and is profoundly painful. I have experienced it watching the deaths of my parents, church members and friends, but the familiarity of the journey never makes it any easier.

The delay in Jesus' arrival, which is so difficult for the sisters, does not have a clear explanation in the text. Tom Wright suggests Jesus is praying in that time, unsure what God's will is in the situation, and that interpretation certainly makes sense.[20] Jesus' humanity, as real as his divinity, meant his knowledge was limited.[21] It does give an opportunity for John to make an interesting distinction in recording the story in his Gospel. The message the sisters send is that 'the one you love is ill',[22] using the word *phileo* – friendship or brotherly love. However, in verse 5, in reporting Jesus' love for this family, it is *agape*, the highest form of love, and the tense is ongoing, suggesting never-ending, unremitting love. They had understood a little of Jesus' love for them, but it was deeper than they realised. What they would discover, however, as we all must, is that being loved by God does not mean an easy time or that everything will go as we want it to, despite some teaching to the contrary, particularly that which rests on an underlying prosperity theology.[23] It is all too easy for us to interpret God's love through our circumstances – 'my health is failing so God does not love me' rather than vice versa – 'my health is failing, but God will hold me in it because of his love'.[24]

It is clear from this story in John 11, as well as from other places[25] that Jesus experienced anger. The verse translated 'he was deeply moved in spirit and troubled'[26] is a curious phrase which denoted a horse snorting and was generally used of anger.[27] It seems that Jesus experienced very real anger at the ravages death caused, certainly in the lives of these sisters, but we may perhaps assume more widely too. Not for nothing is death referred to as 'the last enemy'.[28] It was a stark reminder both of the reality of that enmity, and the costly path he had yet to travel to defeat it.

Our anger is part of the 'flight or fight' system and as such has similarities with anxiety.[29] Our anger triggers a number of bodily changes as adrenaline is released, including a rise in our heart rate and blood pressure. Glucose is released to fuel our body for action, and the release of cortisol depresses the immune system. These and other changes are not usually problematic in the short term, but can be if the anger is not dealt with and our body chemistry remains on high alert.

Anger can be expressed in a number of ways, and not all of them are obvious. One of the most difficult to deal with (which sadly often appears in churches as in other groups of people) is passive aggression. This can be verbal – for example where we experience someone as a 'smiling assassin', saying something profoundly hurtful or unfair but cushioned with phrases such as 'I'm only joking' or 'I'm only saying this to be helpful'. It can also be behavioural, such as the outwardly charming waiter who behind the scenes spits in the food of a difficult customer, or a worker who quietly sabotages a project. This is the most difficult form to deal with since, if challenged, the person will often assume a position of hurt denial.

We are, of course, familiar with more overtly aggressive anger, and it is a huge issue within most societies. It can be terrifying to experience. Some years ago, aged about 20, I was driving with a friend to Cornwall to visit my mother. Someone cut in on us and – perhaps unwisely, but I think from shock at the near miss – my friend flashed his headlights. The car in front slammed on the brakes, leaving us no alternative but to stop. The driver approached our car, not obviously angry and so my friend wound down the window, expecting an apology. In fact, the driver pulled my friend's head through the window by their hair and hit their head repeatedly, leaving us too shocked to take their number plate in order to report it. 'Road rage' is, of course, an established term now and instances, some far more serious, are all too frequent. Often outbreaks of aggression like this are fuelled by feelings of helplessness or stress in other situations (such as home or work) where they cannot be expressed, which results in anger erupting in inappropriate places.

One of the things we need to remember in dealing with our anger is that it is a feeling. This may seem obvious, but is very important. As such I believe it is neutral – it is when the feeling turns into an action, into behaviour, that it has the capacity to become sinful. This is why the apostle Paul can say, as we noted earlier, 'be angry but do not sin' (Eph. 4:26, NRSV). If I feel angry with a driver who takes the parking space I was clearly waiting for, I need to find a way to manage that feeling, but the feeling is not in itself sinful. If, however, I nurse that anger, planning ways I could have humiliated them, or take actual revenge by scratching their car, I would argue that it is at either of those points that I have crossed the line.

Ultimately, there are three ways open to us in dealing with our anger – to repress it, to express it, or to employ it. By repressing anger, I mean any way to hold it in, deny it, or in other ways unhelpfully keep it inside. We are told to be 'slow to become angry',[30] but also warned not to cover it up, which is part of the original meaning of 'do not let the sun go down while you are still angry'.[31] One of the risks of doing that, apart from the physical toll I mentioned above, is that is easily becomes a resentment which eats away at us emotionally and impacts our relationships. It is as though some wild animals are constantly marauding around in our psyche.

Expressing anger, including with tears, can often be helpful, but it needs to be released in the most beneficial way and, if shared, with those who can hear us well. One church leader described to me that when angry in several meetings she had been unable to hold back tears. Instead of giving her time to express what was happening, she was then labelled as weak, forcing her to contain her anger and cry her angry tears in isolation rather than be helped through all that she was experiencing. Anecdotally – I have no research to support this – I suspect women's anger is more often expressed in tears, and men's in some other way.

If we are going to express our anger verbally in the context of a relationship, it is important that we own it as ours – for example saying 'I felt' rather than 'you made me feel'. It is often wise to wait for the immediate surge of anger to have settled to enable us to think out more clearly what we need to say, as well as disentangling what belongs in that relationship from what belongs elsewhere – anger from other situations, or which we carry from the past. We also need a vocabulary that matches the level of our anger. I often used to gently challenge counselling clients who would say 'I am cross' when actually they were livid. One of the helpful things we can do in raising children is help them learn words for all their emotions so that they can both recognise and express them – not just anger, but including it.

The third way is to employ anger, for example in sport, or in social action. Anger can be energising and creative. The adrenaline of anger (or anxiety), if it is not too excessive, can enhance a sporting performance. I have heard, though could not source it, that Mother Teresa once said that what kept her going in the slums of Calcutta was anger – presumably at the devastation wrought by poverty in the lives of those she nursed. Much social reform has come from someone seeing something which made them angry and resolving to do something to change it.

One of the ways we can help ourselves understand our own anger is to consider the 'script' we have picked up about anger from those who cared for us when we were young. These are many and varied – for example 'if I am angry people will not love me' or 'when people get angry bad things happen so I must never get angry'. As I mentioned in the Introduction, I received the message growing up that emotions were to be kept inside, and to me this particularly seemed to apply to anger. I remember on one occasion, aged about 7, I was very angry because I felt I had been rebuked unfairly. I had no idea what to do, or how to express it, so I found a cupboard I could reach and bit the side of it as hard as I could, leaving tooth marks, which fortunately were never noticed. Looking back, it was quite an amusing way to try to deal with it, but I am also left wondering what else I have 'bitten back' over the years. I am trying (with various degrees of success) to learn instead to befriend my anger, to see it as a signal that something is wrong and try to work out what, and address it. I am encouraged in that ongoing quest by the recognition that there is no rebuke from Jesus to Martha for her apparently defiant words, nor to Mary for needing to be called out to see him from what was, perhaps, initially an angry refusal to face him.

I'm aware in writing this chapter that anger is a huge topic, worthy of a book itself, and an area that is problematic for many of us. Aristotle is reputed to have said 'Anybody can become angry, that is easy; but to be angry with the right person, and to the right degree, and at the right time, and for the right purpose, and in the right way, that is not within everybody's power, that is not easy.'[32] God understands, and loves us, and we should never be ashamed to find help if we need it.[33] Don't let it become the monster hiding in your internal wardrobe.[34]

Some questions to reflect on

- When were you last angry? Can you work out why? How did you respond?
- What words do you associate with anger?
- What are some of the messages you have received about anger from others?
- How might you be able to continue to reflect on and potentially befriend or employ your anger? What is the next step for you?

11

Tears of Stress

You know how I lived the whole time I was with
you, from the first day I came into the province
of Asia. I served the Lord with great humility
and with tears and in the midst of severe testing
by the plots of my Jewish opponents.[1]

A current story of tears of stress

Somehow it is never one thing, is it? I should have realised that
the moment was coming, but sometimes I fight against my
humanity, trying to brazen it out in the forlorn and profoundly
counterproductive assumption that if I just plod on, try a little
harder, I will somehow conquer the insurmountable.

So it was that day. I'd been running perilously low on metaphorical petrol for a while – in reality, only wispy vapours
keeping my internal engine ticking over. A holiday was in
sight, time to recoup, so though sailing dangerously close to
the edge, I thought I would just make it to the finish line. I love
my job, but its 24/7 nature, the sense at times that everyone
wants a piece of you and you simply don't have enough, can
stretch compassion even though I genuinely love the people

around me. Family are my greatest joy, but it had been a busy, though delightful, season there too. There were a few health uncertainties and pending tests too, probably ageing, but with the spectre of something potentially more serious, sitting only in the back of my mind, but there nonetheless, like an unwelcome guest who had been relegated to a small attic room but whose footsteps were still echoing disturbingly. My diary had conspired against me – in reality, of course, I had colluded with it, cramming more in than was realistic, rationalising that they were all things I enjoyed. Which was true, but . . .

So that day I had woken with a vague unease, a sense that the list for that day was too long, but silencing it with the thought that if everything went to plan, I could just squeeze it all in and emerge victorious into the evening like a conquering hero.

I nearly managed it, even fitting in a couple of small extra jobs which were unnecessary but faintly pleasing to my sense of potential victory. Just one thing was left, a small job, simply writing out a voucher for a family member, to get it to the post in time for their birthday.

Two things broke my sprint to the finish line. Firstly, an email arrived which indicated that one piece of work I had taken on was going to be much bigger than I had anticipated. I could sense a rising panic, but refused to give in to it, trudging on through the day, just that one card to sort . . .

I couldn't find it. I knew where I had put it safely, at least I thought I did, but it was not there. I searched and searched. Losing a small object has always historically been a tipping point for me, causing me to sometimes spend days searching. I think hugely significant losses early in life have left a vulnerability which oddly finds its expression in small things – perhaps because to access what I feel about the larger losses feels too enormous and frightening.

My searching even included places I knew it could not be. My sense of helplessness ballooned, and somewhere inside I was again a small child in a big world where everything was going wrong and I could not control anything.

So, finally, I gave in, as I should have done weeks before, and the tears came.

Reflecting on the Bible account: Luke's story

It is almost time to board the ship, heading towards Jerusalem. I am watching my friend Paul as he steels himself to say good-bye to our colleagues from Ephesus. I am wondering what they see as they look. Do they see Paul the hero – the leader, the evangelist, the zealot for truth and the gospel? Or, like me, can they see Paul the man, strong yet vulnerable, weary yet determined?

Every line on his weather-beaten face is etched with strain. His eyes are bright, but I see behind them, both as a medic and his companion, a man who has been to the edge of himself. As he begins to speak, and I scan their faces, so my memory takes me back to Ephesus.

I hear many people's stories in my occupation as a doctor. So, you learn to look behind the obvious. It is so easy to view my friend Paul and see him as a conquering champion, powering through Asia with the extraordinary news of Jesus. And that is a very real part of the story. He is indeed an amazing man: I have never met anyone quite like him. He is passionate for the truth – a fervour which led him at first to persecute the followers of Jesus, his anger springing from fear, as is so often the case. He was terrified that they posed a danger to the Judaism that was at the very core of his being and that the foundations of his world – including, but not solely, his hard-earned academic success – would crumble, leaving devastation in their wake. And he had been radically transformed. We had spent many an evening, the preaching for that day complete, with him telling me again the story of that encounter with Jesus on the Damascus road. Sometimes I envied him the certainty springing from that dramatic change: my own discovery of faith had been more gradual and gentle. We are very different, and he carries a determination which his opponents view as fanaticism and his followers as godly zeal. I admire him hugely.

Yet there is much more to him, as there is to us all, and that time in Ephesus was gruelling. Successful, yes, as we saw God do amazing miracles, transforming lives in the most remarkable way. There is nothing as incredible as seeing lives set free as they come to know Jesus as their rescuer.

But the opposition was tough, even terrifying. I still sometimes wake in the night, hearing the roar of that rioting crowd as we held Paul back from the folly of trying to address them. He could easily have ended his days there. The baying pack were beyond control, carried on a wave of hysteria, barely even knowing any longer what had fuelled their anger. He always brazened out opposition – at least on the outside – but I know it cost him dearly. I would see him weep for those who could not see the truth and he carried as a heavy burden the responsibility of sharing the good news of Jesus.

When I write the story, as I will, there are some things I will leave out for the sake of friendship.[2] Another imprisonment, the stench of despair and the constant fear of torture and death. The heavy chains which encircled his soul more than his hands or feet. Hunger gnawing at him day and night and the moments of uncertainty – would God bring him release this time? Had he heard him right about the future still to come?

Then there was the loneliness. That split with Barnabas[3] had cut very deep. Barnabas had been like a father figure to him for many years, encouraging him and bringing out the best, helping Paul see who he could become. I sensed the depth of his hurt as he recounted the story and the sense of helplessness that despite their love for each other they could not put it right. That loss, added to the distance, in every sense, from his spiritual home of Antioch, had left him isolated and somehow unprotected.

As if that were not enough, he became sick again.[4] Unable to work to support himself, or to preach, and unsure of when he would recover, I know he prayed with renewed desperation for God to heal him, but the answer did not come. His body frustrated him – strong as his will was, he could not force strength into his limp limbs or clear his clouded eyes. People are good at supporting for a short time, aren't they, but so few stay for the long haul. Usually in his moments of despair he would grit his teeth and plough on, but now he couldn't and the darkness closed in. He was worn out with worry and sadness.

The final straw, I suspect, was the news from Corinth. Glittering, glorious Corinth, a city which held such outward beauty with its stunning buildings and such inner ugliness and shame, with its depraved lifestyle encouraged by the merchants making money from the temple prostitution in all its foul forms. He had loved those converts as if they were his children, and the news that, chameleon-like, they were sliding back into resembling the culture Jesus had rescued them from devastated him. His compassion was exhausted and yet, like a physical parent whose child has made disastrous decisions which are hurting them, he was also deeply wounded and desperate for them to find their way back. I was saddened as I listened to him describing the pressure he felt. He felt a slave to Jesus, but although at times that was a comfort, at times he felt as dejected as those poor captured souls the Romans would parade in their chains through the streets. He knew there was much that needed to be put to death in him but the dying was an ongoing battle. As a master tentmaker, he longed at times for release from the dwelling of his body, like a tent which had outlived its usefulness and lay in tatters. He held on to the belief that it was all God's grace, yet he was exhausted by the internal voice telling him he needed to try harder. At times, there was nothing I could do but hold him as he wept.

He will find his way back, this my friend. One day he will see himself again as the treasure he is, even though those riches might be encased in the most fragile of containers. Our God will lift him from the dirt.

So I raise my eyes again to him as he makes this sad farewell, looking back and looking ahead to all that waits for him. The lines of stress are still there, but now I see just as clearly the light of bravery and hope which is, even now, stirring in his eyes.

(This account is based on the events in Acts 19 and 20, but set in a wider context.[5])

Stress. On the day I am writing this, if you Google the word you get 'about' (Google's word) 1,660,000,000 hits. That's a lot of writing about stress. Amusingly, as I sat down to write this section my stress levels were definitely rising as issues with the computer, or the internet, were preventing me from doing a simple job I wanted done so that I could concentrate on writing.

At first glance, it is easy to make a simplistic assumption about stress that it is always a negative thing, something to be eliminated at all cost. However, that is not true. Also, today as I sit here there are several major sporting events happening in various places. An athlete who is too relaxed, with no pre-race or match nerves, may well not perform as well. Back in 1908, two psychologists, Robert M. Yerkes and John Dillingham Dodson, proposed the imaginatively titled Yerkes-Dodson law. Depicted as a bell-shaped graph, this law suggests that up to a certain point, arousal (the underlying mechanism of stress) will increase performance and productivity. After a certain point, however, there will be a decline. There are at least two variables that determine when that change from helpful to unhelpful takes place. One is the task – for example, a task requiring mental concentration will be easier with less arousal, whereas one which is based on physical stamina may benefit from more. The other factor is the individual. Individual responses to stress vary a great deal. Some of it is personality – any parent of several children, brought up as identically as possible, will comment on how different those children can be in levels of sensitivity to pressure. As we will see shortly, there are a great variety of triggers for stress ('stressors') which people will experience very differently. Life experiences will also impact us, including the way we have observed our caregivers responding to difficult situations.

So, what exactly is stress? In the physical realm, of course, metals will be subjected to a 'stress test' where pressure is exerted on the item to ensure it can withstand it. In the realm of human biology and psychology, at its simplest, stress is the response to pressure from a situation, life event, or a combination of circumstances. There are many issues commonly cited when people report stress – for example, jobs, money, difficulty in relationships, or the sheer multiplicity of tasks. Something which begins as a pressure tips over into stress when we feel that the resources we have – whether material or emotional – are not enough to cope with the challenges we face, and when the result of that assessment creates fear in us, or leads us to feel that the situation is out of control and we feel helpless.

What is clear is that stress, whatever its cause, results in physical effects in our bodies. This is because we have what is called the 'flight or fight' response, which we also considered in Chapter 7, when we looked at fear. To recap, faced with immediate danger the body will respond with an increase in adrenaline, raising our heart rate, blood pressure and pulse and redirecting blood to key muscles and the brain and away from less urgently needed functions such as digestion. This allows us to decide if flight or fight is the best option. This is very useful when we are in imminent danger, and when the threat is over, the body returns to normal. However, it becomes problematic if either we perceive there is danger when there isn't, or where we have a number of prolonged situations where the body never has a chance to restore 'normal settings'.

Hans Selye (1907–82) was an endocrinologist (someone who studies hormones and related diseases) and I suspect that most of those reading this book have not heard of him, although he received numerous awards, including being nominated several times for a Nobel Prize. He discovered and coined the term General Adaption Syndrome – which describes how stress produces certain hormonal reactions, which if they remain at high levels in the body, result in physical illnesses. He later admitted the word 'strain' might have been better. This difficulty with vocabulary still plagues us, as 'stress' can sometimes be used of the cause – more accurately, the stressor – and at other times of the result, what we feel and experience.

These chemical changes he studied are the reason prolonged stress can lead to a number of physical illnesses, such as high blood pressure, thyroid problems and various digestive conditions, as well as emotional difficulties such as problems with concentration, intrusive negative thoughts etc. Over time this can translate into behaviours – avoiding tasks or people, changes in sleeping patterns, increased use of alcohol or other substances, and eating differently – I eat more when under stress, others find themselves unable to eat. And of course, given the topic of this book – we can respond with tears. They are helpful in releasing short-lived tension, but if we find ourselves crying excessively and uncontrollably over a sustained period, that may be a sign that we need to address the stress we are under.

Stress can be caused by factors which are external, internal, or both. One of the major sources of external stressors is our life circumstances. In 1967, Holmes and Rahe developed a questionnaire to identify life events which are stressful, having looked through medical records to find a correlation between life events and illness.[6] I've always resisted completing the questionnaire since if it highlighted a risk of illness that would only add to my stress. However, it has been helpful in bringing to general attention that life events do impact us enormously, especially if they come together. It is not a perfect list – for example, they rate death of a spouse as the most stressful, whereas I would place the death of a child as equally so (in the scale that comes under 'close family member' at number five). It also ranks death of a friend at seventeen, whereas that can be devastating where friends have spent a great deal of time together and have shared deeply. It is helpful, however, in also recognising that even happy events, such as marriage and the birth of children, contribute to stress. Many life events on the list involve bereavement, and of course any change, however welcome, involves loss – the birth of a baby, for example, whilst usually celebrated, involves the loss of freedoms (and sleep!).

Paul's life was littered with stressful incidents. He describes it in one letter in the following words:

> Five times I received from the Jews the forty lashes minus one. Three times I was beaten with rods, once I was pelted with stones, three times I was shipwrecked, I spent a night and a day in the open sea, I have been constantly on the move. I have been in danger from rivers, in danger from bandits, in danger from my fellow Jews, in danger from Gentiles; in danger in the city, in danger in the country, in danger at sea; and in danger from false believers. I have laboured and toiled and have often gone without sleep; I have known hunger and thirst and have often gone without food; I have been cold and naked. Besides everything else, I face daily the pressure of my concern for all the churches.[7]

What a list of stressors.

Some stressors, however, are internal. Our personalities impact our capacity for dealing with stress. People who are competitive, ambitious, or naturally anxious may well be more inclined to experience stress. Whilst our external circumstances are highly significant, our interpretation of them impacts our response. If, for example, a person's sense of self-worth and identity is centred chiefly around work life, then challenges in that area will have much more effect than it will on someone who sees work as important but not defining.

Our personal histories will also make a difference in our battles with stress. If we have received overprotective parenting it may be more challenging for us to develop the resilience needed under stress: we may experience a kind of learned helplessness and look to others rather than harnessing our own resources.

However, even the most resilient person, if subjected to a high enough number of stressors for long enough, will begin to be negatively impacted. So, what can we do if we find ourselves beginning to drown? This book is not a manual for stress – there are many useful resources, some of which are at the end of the book, but here are a few brief thoughts.

The first step is to try to understand its origins. What are the life events which have occurred over the last few months? Recently I was talking to someone who was feeling stressed and tearful. As I asked her to describe the last few months, it became clear there had been a number of losses, by death but also in other ways. As I pointed this out, I could sense the relief as her stress was explained and normalised and she immediately felt more able to deal with it.

The second step is practical. Are we getting enough sleep? Is there a healthy pattern of work and rest – the Sabbath principle, which is a really key command in Scripture?[8] I meet many Christians who struggle to rest, putting heavy demands on themselves, which are sometimes based on an underlying belief, despite the New Testament emphasis on grace, that God's love has to be earned. Yes, Christians believe we are called to lay down our lives in submission to God, but not to overwork ourselves in a driven way for the kingdom. 'Be still, and know that I am God'[9] literally means stop striving. I love the way *The Message* phrases Jesus' words: 'Are you tired? Worn out? Burned out on religion? Come to me. Get away with me and you'll recover your life. I'll show you how to take a real rest. Walk with me and work with me – watch how I do it. Learn the unforced rhythms of grace. I won't lay anything heavy or ill-fitting on you. Keep company with me and you'll learn to live freely and lightly.'[10] Equally practical is the need to watch our eating habits (sugary foods spike the blood sugar but it can then crash, beginning a vicious circle), and our alcohol intake (alcohol induces sleep but then has the opposite effect a few hours later, apart from the other hazards of overindulgence).

The third step is to address our thinking. Under stress we can catastrophise – think only in worst-case scenarios which can paralyse our efforts to address the stressful situation. We can also think globally, in the sense that one incident – such as failing at a task – becomes an overarching 'fact', so we tell ourselves, 'I am a failure.' I had a previous boss who would often say to people 'You are not a failure. You are a child of God who sometimes fails.' There is a huge difference between the two. Changing our perceptions of a situation can be enormously helpful, and why sometimes cognitive behavioural therapy (CBT)[11] can be really effective, teaching skills such as challenging negative thinking. It can be useful to ask those we trust to tell us what strengths they see in us. We need to remember that we are human, not perfect.

A final factor in dealing with stress, which I don't think is mentioned enough, is our sense of humour (which needs to be distinguished from flippancy, which can be defensive). It is a really helpful personality trait in dealing with stress. Laughter is increasingly being recognised as having physical as well as mental and social benefits, triggering the release of endorphins ('feel-good' chemicals and natural pain relievers), and boosting the immune system. Weakening of the immune system is increasingly being seen as a factor in the development of a number of illnesses[12] and its importance is also being explored in various treatments, such as immunotherapy. Whilst the benefit of laughter undoubtedly has a physical element, it also allows a reframing of the stressful situation – for example, seeing it or ourselves differently – which also has the potential to reduce stress. I know several people who under stress watch comedy and find it very helpful.

And yes, when we need to, we can allow our tears to help us.

Some questions to reflect on

- Can you remember when you were last stressed? What did it feel like? You might want to write words, or to draw a picture to describe it.
- What less helpful behaviours are you drawn to when stressed?
- What are the things which help you when you are stressed?
- Are there any aspects of your lifestyle or thinking which, if you address them, might increase your resilience under stress?

Part Two

Further Thoughts

12

Tears Seen by God

. . . she thought, 'I cannot watch the boy die.'
And as she sat there, she began to sob.

God heard the boy crying, and the angel of God
called to Hagar from heaven and said to her,
'What is the matter, Hagar? Do not be afraid;
God has heard the boy crying as he lies there. Lift
the boy up and take him by the hand . . .'[1]

A current story of tears seen by God

Sometimes it feels as though your tears will be endless. A while
ago I entered one of those phases, and I thought it would never
finish. A series of family difficulties which caused me enormous distress had echoes with events from my past and so
had brought me to a place of unspeakable pain. This pain was
magnified because the things that were happening now opened
scars which I thought had healed. Now they were not only
reopened, but raw again.

Although I fought the tears, at times they came unbidden
and threatened to spill over into the public persona which I so

carefully cultivated: cheerful, resilient and able to glide above circumstances with the grace of a swan. Very few had seen the under-the-water scrabbling to keep upright and, wary of deeply trusting others, I was happy to keep it that way.

A friend, though, was not fooled, and so I began to quietly open up some of the hidden places in my past and present, sometimes in a walk round the park, at other times in emails, as my feelings somehow seemed easier for me to write than voice. I'm so grateful for their patience, over a long time.

Yet the most difficult part of all was that God seemed silent. I would cry out to him but the heavens seemed shut tight. At times the tears rolled quietly down, at other times the sobs were desperate, torn from a deep place inside, leaving my throat and soul raw and sore. Yet still there was nothing from God. Zilch. *Nada.* I wasn't angry, just bewildered. It seemed as though God had led me into the wilderness and simply left me there. That apparently mute response was as painful as the events which had engulfed me, perhaps more so. It was as though I was invisible and he was deaf.

I was a seasoned Christian. I knew the theoretical responses. 'God is with us', nothing 'will be able to separate us from the love of God'[2] . . . but at that time it simply did not cut it. They seemed to be just empty words, bouncing off the hard edges of my reality.

Then, in one of the email exchanges, my friend said simply that God weeps with me – that in the silence he was shedding tears. Somehow that made the tiniest bit of sense, a glimmer of the light of hope among the darkness. On another occasion he said that God spoke about me to his angels with tears in his eyes, boasting at my faithfully continuing despite the darkness.

As I reflected on what he said, I realised slowly that there was more than simple kindness there. Jesus himself was a man of tears. He wept at the tomb of his friend Lazarus[3] even though he was about to raise him from the dead. He wept over Jerusalem, seeing ahead to its destruction a few decades later.[4] The letter to the Hebrews says, 'During the days of Jesus' life on earth, he offered up prayers and petitions with fervent cries and tears to the one who could save him from death',[5] perhaps a reference to tears he shed in the Garden of Gethsemane. We may safely assume there were other occasions – Jesus was free to feel and show all his emotions in a way we are not; part of our brokenness is that our feelings become trapped and often need coaxing into expression.

It says in the Old Testament that 'The LORD your God is with you, the Mighty Warrior who saves. He will take great delight in you; in his love he will no longer rebuke you, but will rejoice over you with singing.'[6] If God sings in joy over us, I began to think that it might make sense that he weeps over us too, in a way that Jesus was able to bodily express. Jeremiah 14:17 speaks of the tears of God for his people.

A neat Christian ending would be good here, wouldn't it? Instant healing, the return of joy. It wasn't like that, and isn't still. That period of intense darkness gradually, almost imperceptibly, moved into another phase, at first resembling twilight and then periodic daylight. The tears became less, the sense of abandonment diminished. Yet I still know sadness, and sometimes they flow again. And I have to return again to that hope – that when God is silent, he is weeping with me with a sorrow that is beyond, and more truly expressive than, words.

Reflecting on the Bible account: Hagar's story

The enmity of two women. That is how it began, and how it ended. Two women who were unequally matched and whose future was inextricably linked with one powerful yet acquiescent man. Two women who could have come together in mutual help but who instead turned their backs on each other with disastrous consequences. But in the end, perhaps we both won. I'm not sure.

It all began when I was taken from Egypt. At first, I did not mind: the family seemed fair though they never really looked at me or called me by name. I was just there, a nonentity to fulfil their needs. But there was food and water, and a life of sorts. I even felt sorry for my mistress, her ageing body refusing to give her the child she clearly longed for. Sometimes I heard them arguing, something to do with a promise from their God, and I could hear the desperation in her voice.

But that was before she came to me, told me that she had a plan. I was to go to my master, a kind of second wife, to see if I could bear him the child that her barrenness was robbing them of. A son, of course. I saw the mix of feelings in her eyes: failure, regret, hope and a myriad of other unspoken emotions vying with her need to fix this, to come up with a strategy, however unsavoury it might be to her. She still did not look directly at me or, I suspect, think about my place in it at all. It was all about giving Abram[7] what he wanted. I wondered if they had asked their God what he thought about the idea. They certainly never invited me to say what I felt.

So, I did as I was instructed, and found he did not see me, either, except as the potential bearer of his heir. My body did as they demanded and my mind went to another place. I don't think I had ever felt so alone.

I sensed at once that I was going to bear a child. Sometimes we women do. As the days moved on to weeks and the subtle changes in my body became more marked, I became sure. I hoped they would be pleased, but somehow my burgeoning body seemed to damage even further the fragile relationship between us women, reminding Sarai of her childlessness and me of the callous way they had used me. The very thing she thought would build her up[8] had made her feel smaller, and I had just been the means to their end and so was even less a person both in her eyes and my own – just a walking womb to bear the child, who would be theirs not mine. We drifted into a mutual contempt which I was forced to hide, but which she made no attempt to.

So, I felt I had no choice. As both the situation and my increasing sense of isolation became unbearable, I ran away. What else can a slave do? As they slept, I headed out into the wilderness. It was dark and cold, but no more so than in the camp and in my heart. I set off for the only other home I had experienced – Egypt – although with no clear plan what I would do when I arrived, and frightened that I would be punished as a deserting slave. But I was *not* going to stay where I was invisible, would *not* be the victim to their selfishness. I was going to decide my own future. I would speak with my actions what I could not say with my words. They could not enslave me.

Enough distance between us to feel safe, I stopped at a spring. Reality began to overtake me. I was alone and defenceless, at the mercy of both wild animals and men. What would become of me and the child I was carrying? I began to shiver as my plight hit home.

At first it seemed as though my fears had been somehow embodied as I looked up with a start to see a man standing there. Instinctively I put my hand on my stomach in an involuntary if futile attempt to both disguise and protect the child I was carrying.

But then this mysterious stranger spoke. More than that, he looked at me, really looked, and then spoke to me by name – I almost did not recognise it, since I had not been addressed by it in so long: 'Hagar . . . where have you come from, and where are you going?'[9] For the briefest of moments my mind raced through the past, and the future was a blank, so I could not answer his question other than the stark truth of the present – that I was running away.

'You need to get back there.' His words voiced the truth that had been slowly melting my reckless desire to play the heroine. I could hardly return to Egypt, pregnant and alone. Yet before I could take that in, before my hope could be extinguished in the growing harsh light of reality as dawn rose over the wilderness, he gave me a promise. Descendants beyond measure – a family at last. I saw myself not alone by this remote spring, but surrounded by the future, held in the arms of the new life growing within as much as he would be held in mine. Ishmael – God listens, hears, pays attention. He was to be a feisty and rugged survivor. My son, not theirs. The tough return ahead would only be part of our story.

I knew this was no ordinary man. I knew somehow that the God they had spoken of was real, and had chosen to come and find me to help me discover him. So boldly I decided to name him 'the God who sees me'.[10] He saw me, and then I saw him.

So, I went back. No option, really, but I clung onto the promise, cherished the thought that I was not invisible to their God even though I continued to be to them. My son was born, named and grew. I would whisper to him of both the future and the hope I held for us.

Fourteen years passed, and against all my expectations Sarai gave birth to a son. She had despised us when she had no son, and now she despised us when she did. This time I was sent back into the wilderness, my master giving me all the food and water I could carry, as if to salve his conscience. It was never going to be enough, and his eyes were downcast as if with shame as he handed it to me. I was being sent into exile.

Before long I was lost, and realised I was repeatedly circling the same section of this desert. Soon both the food and water ran out. I squeezed the last drop into Ishmael's parched mouth, gently wiping his cracked lips and holding him to my breasts, dried up years ago and with nothing now to offer him. Spent, I had no way to save him, or even to ease his passing. As he became sleepy for lack of sustenance, I placed him under a tree for shade and walked away to curl up and sob in helpless desperation, at a distance both so that my cries would not wake him and because I could no longer bear to watch my bright and vibrant boy slowly slipping into the valley of shadows and away from me. What good were those promises now?

I heard him stir, and begin to cry softly, like the mewing of an animal with no strength left even to protest. I knew I had to go back to him, to hold him on that last journey, yet my limbs would not move. It was then I heard a voice, different from all those years before, yet somehow the same. 'What's the matter?' A fury shot through me. If this is the all-seeing God paying me another visit, why does his messenger need to ask the blindingly obvious? Before I could retort he continued. 'Do not be afraid; God has heard the boy crying'.[11]

Even before he finished speaking, I knew. My son would not die but that promise from years ago was, despite everything, going to come true. I looked up, and there was the water my despair and my tears had hidden from sight.

Our tears were, after all, seen, our cries heard, by God. We were going to live.

(Hagar's story is found in Genesis 16:1–16 and 21:9–21.)

As I sat down to write this chapter, two memories from my childhood and adolescence came to mind. The first was one I mentioned in the chapter on friendship, from the time that I was about 7. I used to hide under a camellia bush in our garden which was very old and of sufficient size that it could completely shield a small child. I did not want to be seen.

In the second, from my teenage years, I was with a group of friends exploring the beauty of the Cornish coast. I had experienced a number of losses and was struggling to process them. Having been taught inadvertently to suppress what I felt, I had not been able to explain to my friends how deeply distressed I was. So, sometimes I would walk away a little, bodily expressing my sense of isolation, yet in the hope that someone would notice and come to find me. I wanted to be seen – really seen. I can't recall now if anyone ever did.

At times – such as when I was small – we don't want to be seen. Some reasons are innocuous ones, such as planning a surprise. Others centre around the fear of being caught, whether due to some childhood misdemeanour after which we are hoping to be spared the resulting punishment, or even being engaged in criminal activity where the repercussions of detection are more serious. Sometimes, sadly, we seek invisibility because of fear, such as is experienced by someone living in a home where there is violence or abuse. These and other painful life experiences can lead us to be very cautious in letting people see what lies underneath the public face we wear. It can take real courage to share our stories, to take off the masks and allow ourselves to be vulnerable – to be seen as we really are, not just as the labels people give us or the superficial judgements we make about each other.[12] It is so much easier to hide in the shadows. There are also different ways to be seen. I get up most Sundays and talk to a large group of people and whilst I am always nervous, aware as I am of the responsibility, it is quite different from the profound uneasiness and embarrassment I feel if the spotlight is on me personally rather than the message I am trying to bring.

However, alongside these exceptions there is within us a deep need to be seen. As I type this, the Rugby World Cup Final is about to be played. In television coverage of any sport, the moment people spot the camera is on their section of the crowd, most of them leap up and down and generally try to become as visible as possible. People in their millions post their selfies on social media.

Being seen is, of course, much more than someone seeing our picture or noticing that we are there. How often have you had a conversation with someone when you knew they were not really present? This might be shown by them not really making eye contact, perhaps distracted by their phone or looking elsewhere, or simply not being able or willing to take the time to grasp what you are saying, their eyes glazing over. Skilled listeners convey a deep sense of presence, of really being with someone, and it is a precious gift to give another person. In the Genesis account, Abram and Sarai never use Hagar's name – she is just referred to as their slave. She is marginalised and never speaks. She seems to be neither really seen nor heard by her master and mistress, and this is one of the things which makes the wilderness meeting so significant. Before it, she is at best objectified for their purposes and at worst silenced by abuse. At the spring, she is spoken to, addressed by name, and finds her voice, all for the first time since her enslavement. In doing so, and in naming God, she becomes the Bible's first theologian.[13] If, as various writers suggest, theology is often born out of pain,[14] this extraordinary woman's story, in many ways so tragic, was the first biblical occasion when suffering gave birth to a new understanding of God. It was not to be the last.

Various psychologists have helped to underline the significance of our being seen and heard. Abraham Maslow is best known for his hierarchy of needs.[15] Usually depicted as a pyramid, in which the lower essentials must be met in order that those above can also be experienced, he described five basic needs: physiological (food, water etc.), safety, belonging and love, social needs/esteem and self-actualisation. The need to be seen and heard, really understood, comes as part of both the need for belonging and love, and of self-esteem.

The work of Eric Berne, founder of Transactional Analysis, can help us further understand this need to be seen.[16] Using the perhaps misleading term 'strokes', he describes the craving for social recognition in all of us. He had been influenced by René Spitz, an Austrian-American psychoanalyst who studied child development and particularly the negative effect on children of not being physically touched and held – hence the use of the term 'strokes'. Berne argued that we carry that same need for recognition into adulthood, but that it usually takes a different form – a smile, compliment, hand gesture and so on. Perhaps it helps to think about what happens at the supermarket checkout – if the cashier looks at us and smiles, we feel much better than if they just push things through without any social contact – we have received a positive non-verbal stroke. If they frown, we have received a negative non-verbal stroke. If they ask us how our day is, it is a positive verbal stroke, and so on.

Berne describes this need in both children and adults as 'recognition hunger'.[17] He also theorised that any recognition is better than none – which goes part way to explaining why children who are being ignored behave badly; at least then they receive 'negative strokes', which is better than none at all.

If ever someone suffered recognition hunger it must have been Hagar in the first part of the story in Genesis 16. What a contrast then to receive the promises of a future – 'positive strokes' at last. They are even more remarkable when we consider she is the first woman to be given a personal, direct promise from and by God for a child, and the last before Mary receives her unique annunciation.[18] Later on in Genesis 21 come the 'negative strokes' of rejection and exile – the threats to her emotional and physical survival are equally real and the lack of a refreshing spring a powerful metaphor as well as a physical reality.

This need to be seen is universal, not linked to personality types. While introverts need time alone or with one other person to recharge their emotional batteries, they have the same need for recognition as an extrovert who will be energised by a party. It is common to us all, no matter how differently it may need to be experienced. Clearly, the less we have received appropriate care in childhood, the more desperately we may crave what we have been deprived of. This may lead to us seeking it either in unhelpful ways, such as inappropriate attention-seeking or manipulation, or places which are not ultimately beneficial, such as relationships which offer us something short term but have no future or are damaging. The old saying about children being seen and not heard is nonsense. If we are not heard, we are not really seen either: we need both.

This need for recognition, to be seen, has interesting implications for the workplace. Some fascinating research[19] by Dan Ariely, Emir Kamenica and Drazen Prelec looked at the importance of being acknowledged. Participants were given a repetitive task, and when they returned the results to the researchers, were either acknowledged (by the researcher looking up, scanning the results and filing them), were ignored (by the researcher not looking up and simply filing it away), or the results were shredded, again without the researcher looking up. The researchers looked at how long the participants would continue with the task – the participants were expecting payment depending on output. It was found that the group who were acknowledged persisted for approximately a third longer than both the other groups; interestingly, there was no difference between those who were ignored and the results filed and those who were ignored and the paper shredded. The only difference was in the group where the researcher looked up before filing. It seems ignoring someone at work impacts hugely on their motivation, and is more significant than the attention paid to their actual work, or even monetary gain.

So, to be seen, and understood, is key to our wellbeing, and this is particularly the case in times of difficulty. The theme of God hearing cries of pain and seeing suffering is a strong one in the Bible. Hagar's story is the first time it is mentioned, but it won't be the last. Years later Hagar's nation of Egypt becomes a place of great oppression for the Jewish people, generations after they had sought sanctuary there in famine.[20] In the story of Moses' wilderness period after he has to flee Egypt, the narrator makes clear that God has heard the cries of the Israelites.[21] When God speaks during Moses' call to action at the burning bush, he says: 'I have indeed seen the misery of my people in Egypt. I have heard them crying out because of their slave drivers, and I am concerned about their suffering. So I have come down to rescue them . . .'[22] There are no easy answers to the problem of suffering – indeed, we might well argue no answers at all. But the belief that God is not immune to our pain – that he sees it, hears every cry and cares deeply about it, can be of great comfort to people of faith.

A couple of years ago, a friend of mine was diagnosed with motor neurone disease. It is a devastating disease which takes different forms in different people but this fit, relatively young woman was soon wheelchair-bound and needing a ventilator to aid her breathing. While she was still able to get to church despite this debilitation, she attended an evening service where the sermon was on the passage from Exodus 3. This idea of God seeing and hearing the distress she was experiencing, that it mattered to him, struck a deep chord and she reflected on it often. It was not a solution or a sinecure, and rescue did not come in the form she might have hoped. She battled with faith until her death, simultaneously holding onto it and asking profound, and sometimes angry, questions. But knowing that God was not immune, that he saw and heard, made an enormous difference in those last brave months.

Some questions to reflect on

- Who are the people in your life who have really heard and seen you? If you are still in contact with them, why not thank them for how important that was?
- Are there any times in your life when you have felt that you have not been seen or heard? If it is still difficult to think about, or you are feeling that now, it might be good to find someone you can share your story with.
- Are you ever too busy to really 'see' others? Who can you take time to really acknowledge this week?
- What difference might it make to believe that God sees your tears, and hears your weeping?

13

Unshed Tears

Then the Philistines seized him, gouged out his eyes and took him down into Gaza.[1]

A current story of unshed tears

My mam died when I was 13, very suddenly and tragically whilst on holiday with her mother, aunts and sisters. They were in Oberammergau visiting the 1970 Passion Play. She had a stroke the day before coming home and died two weeks later. She was just 42.

I am one of eight children and while she was away my dad had taken two weeks off work to look after the six of us left at home – the other two were married. On the day Mam had the stroke, my dad had kept me and my twin sister off school to give the house a good tidy up ready for her coming home.

In the afternoon my sister and I were upstairs doing the bedrooms when we saw our doctor pull up outside. My dad went out to him. The doctor spoke to him and we could see my dad slump. The doctor gave him tablets out of his bag and, we discovered later, said he would be back as soon as he had more news. He was our only contact with the family in Austria.

My dad came in and we ran down the stairs. He was sitting sobbing in the living room. We had never seen my dad cry and we were totally confused and frightened. He gave us money to go to the phone box down the road and we had to ring our older sisters and get them to come home. We had to tell them our mam had taken ill and was not coming home the next day.

At the phone box I was struggling not to cry so I could make the phone calls. My twin was a wreck and couldn't cope with the situation so I had to take charge, even though all I wanted to do was scream in sheer panic.

Both sisters screamed on being told the news, then yelled questions which I couldn't answer, all behaviour I just wasn't used to or could handle. We ran home and the neighbours had started coming round, which was a relief as they took charge for us. I did not cry, even though it was all I wanted to do. I did realise that not crying wasn't right, but I think now it was the shock, and a sense of responsibility for the others.

A week later we were told that my mam had made a slight improvement and so she might be able to be brought home. The days leading up to this message were an emotional rollercoaster as we had very little information from Austria. Still I had no tears. In fact, because we were the subject of talk in the neighbourhood, I began to feel embarrassed about everything and started to shut down any uncomfortable thoughts and feelings and just didn't talk about it any more. I guess it was easier than to open up and deal with the emotions that didn't sit easily with me.

At this point I went on a planned holiday with close family friends. I felt reassured by the news of the improvement, so felt happy and lifted in spirit.

Whilst on the holiday, which started on the Friday, I remember that I thought about my mam each night when going to bed. On the Monday night, 29 June, I was getting into bed when an overwhelming thought, or message perhaps, came to me which told me my mam had died. I accepted the thought and knew deep in my heart it was true. My reaction was to shut off and I went to sleep without mentioning it to the family I was with.

As the end of the holiday approached, I knew I was going home to be told the sad news, and that's what happened. She had died on 28 June, but my family, because of the poor communication, were only told on the 29th in the evening. I cannot explain how I knew while on that holiday, but I do know it helped prepare me for what I was coming back to.

When I got home, all my siblings were out and my dad and aunt were there. The living room curtains were closed even though it was the afternoon, a sign of a family death. As I walked into the house, my dad went straight upstairs and my aunt showed me a newspaper cutting telling the story of my mam's tragic death. I did not cry. My family had all been together when the news was brought, they had cried and hugged together. No tears, no affection, no grieving for me.

For nearly three decades my tears stayed uncried. My real grief finally came, out of the blue, when I was 42. I hadn't realised at the time the relevance of my age. I cried and cried and cried. I was exhausted, overwhelmed and confused. How could this be . . . nearly thirty years late? A counsellor later told me that grief has no time limit. All those years of thinking I was strong because I never cried . . . how wrong could I have been. Finding this release became a life-changer for me.

Reflecting on the Bible account: Samson's story

I have no tears to cry. Everything in me longs to weep, but I can't. All I can do is remember, and it is breaking my heart.

It is a heavy burden to be a special child. To have been prayed for, longed for, promised for service to God before taking your first breath. My parents would tell me often, seeing it as something that would help me stand tall, but instead all I felt was the weight of expectation that my puny emotional shoulders were too weak to bear. I stumbled under the load. In every way. I was so strong, yet so pathetic. At times I saw the sadness in my mother's eyes as she grieved for the man I had become.

We all carry a weakness, don't we? For me it was always women. Their soft skin, their eyes so innocent yet wise, the vulnerability and yet the strength they carry. How I long now for a woman's gentle touch, but that is lost for ever. Even from a young age I loved easily, but not wisely. Somehow my frailty sat alongside God's Spirit within me in a deeply uneasy alliance. I can still remember my parents' disappointment that first time that I had fallen for someone who was not from our people. I hadn't even spoken to her but I wanted her, and I was determined to get my own way.

It frightened me, that day I killed the lion. I knew it was a strength beyond what I possessed and I felt fear for the future. It was foolish in a way to set that riddle to my enemies – almost a goad. I knew the Law – I should never have gone back to the carcass; touching dead things is forbidden and that's why I never told my parents where the honey had come from. And in the end my wife was loyal to her people . . . not to me. That woman could cry, unlike me now, eyeless here in Gaza. A whole week she sobbed, begging me to tell her. She had her reasons, I know, but in the end it cost me dearly that I couldn't resist her tears. So much anger, so much destruction and yet still I did not learn.

Delilah. Ah, beautiful, beguiling Delilah. Even now I can't hate her. Sleeping like a baby in her lap while my strength was taken from me. Those few moments of blissful peace before my whole world came crashing down. My hair was not as many supposed a testament to my vanity, but a symbol of my fragile hold on my vow to God. My strength gone, I found myself grinding grain like the women I had once loved, circling unseeing as one day turned pointlessly to another. I'm like a shorn lion tied to an altar to their god.

And now I stand, my calloused hands on the wood of the pillars of this great hall where they have brought me for their sport as they bring their sacrifice. I've been led like a child by a child, hearing their celebration, their arrogant crowing at my demise, my ears echoing with their hollow worship of a pagan god. As I sense around my face the touch of my renewed hair I wonder too if God will take me back, if there is one last chance for me to show the dedication which has always eluded me, not because I deserve it but because he is merciful. So, I pray, as I have not done for a long time, a faltering prayer because I long ago ran out of words as well as tears. Perhaps, this last deed done, I can finally go home.

(For Samson's story, see Judges 13 – 16.)

Throughout this book I have been trying to honour tears: to normalise them as part of what makes us truly human, and even more than that, to see them as biblical and, at times, a gift of the Spirit. So, what about when the tears won't come? One person described his difficulty in this way: 'I can't remember the last time I cried. I don't cry in films. I don't cry reading the paper. I didn't cry when I saw my son's school photograph. Or even when I held them in their first few minutes on earth. I didn't cry just now when I tried to apologise to my wife. I don't think it's macho or manly. I feel the opposite to that. I think it creates empathy and takes vulnerability. I think it can help make a man. I don't do it on purpose. I don't hold it in. It's not that I don't feel things . . . I could cry with joy, cry with confusion, cry with pain, cry with hope, cry off my demons, cry deeper into love. But I don't.'

I have been honest about the ambivalent relationship with my own tears, and I suspect I am not the only one. This may be particularly so in the culture I live in, the UK. One of the fundamental factors in our ability to shed tears freely and without shame is undoubtedly our cultural surroundings and the prevailing or assumed attitudes to feelings and their expression.

The attitude of the British to emotion is in reality more complex than national caricatures might suggest. In fact, even the word 'emotion' is relatively new. Historically, what we term emotions were understood in terms of 'humours' – blood, phlegm, yellow bile and black bile, the imbalance of which was thought to be the cause of all diseases, as described, among other places, in the writing of Hippocrates. Their imbalance was also thought to be at the root of our personalities: a surfeit of black bile, for example, being responsible for melancholy. Thomas Dixon, in his 2016 book, *Weeping Britannia*[2] traces the attitude of British people to tears historically, making clear that the cultural norm in these islands was not always to suppress emotion.

However, for whatever reason, the propensity to hold our emotions back, including tears, is clearly there within the national psyche. We speak of a 'stiff upper lip', taken from the tendency of our mouths to quiver under strong emotion, particularly tears. Interestingly, perhaps ironically, this phrase originates in America, being used there before later being used in the UK.[3] At times disguising our feelings is specifically

associated with heroism – for example in recounting how
Captain Lawrence Oates, aware that his health was compro-
mising the survival of his companions, walked quietly out into
the night. And what about that phrase, originating in 1939
and now with variations on hundreds of mugs: 'Keep calm and
carry on'? I was amused to find one which said 'Keep calm and
fake a British accent'! There are on the internet, sadly, images
of a wide variety of variations of 'Keep calm and don't cry'.

Whatever the complex history culturally here in Britain,
there appears to remain within many people a deep shame
about tears. I have lost count of the occasions when someone in
a situation of real grief and pain has apologised to me for crying. Though I have spent my working life as a counsellor and
then minister assuring people that tears are not only normal
but beneficial, if I find myself in tears with a colleague or even
a friend, I find myself saying sorry and looking for reassurance
that my tears are acceptable. The language we use does not
help – we speak about 'breaking down', 'having a meltdown',
or 'losing it'. I would be interested to know whether these
potentially pejorative phrases exist in other languages spoken
in nations where emotion is more freely expressed. As I com-
mented in the chapter on loss, if someone 'holds it together' at
a funeral we might speak of them 'doing well', despite the fact
that, as the first story above illustrates, withholding our tears is
usually not ultimately helpful.

It has been argued, I think with some veracity, that a change
is beginning to be seen in our attitudes in this country. None of
us alive at the time can forget the national outpouring of grief
when Diana, Princess of Wales, died in 1997. I can remember
reflecting that since she was not personally known to the vast
majority of people who were responding with weeping as they
laid flowers, this was perhaps giving them an outlet for grief

that belonged to other experiences in their lives. Sportspeople now often show emotion freely – joy in winning, tears in defeat. Even our politicians occasionally show emotion, such as when Theresa May resigned in 2019.

Mentioning Mrs May leads me to another factor in our relationship with tears – the attitudes to gender and crying. She herself whilst in post was the victim of ambivalent attitudes to women's emotions; if she was resolute, her presentation was described as robotic. Women who cry can be perceived as weak – potentially a real difficulty in some workplaces – but if they don't, they are seen as hard. Men, on the other hand, can be socialised into believing that some of their feelings are unacceptable – 'big boys don't cry'. However, if a feeling is not expressed, it does not mean it is not present. It may find a different form; for example, sadness may emerge as anger, which may, depending on how it is expressed, seem more acceptable. With suppressed emotions, when they are finally released, they can be alarming both to the person and to those around because of both their unfamiliarity and their ferocity. Inevitably, as always with comments about gender, there is some generalisation here, but anecdotal evidence and some research[4] shows it is a valid observation, at least in the UK and Europe, where most of the studies have been conducted.

Undoubtedly another very significant factor in our ability to express our emotion, including tears, is that of our family background. In my own family, as I have indicated, I received a very mixed message. My mother did not express her emotions – I cannot remember ever seeing her cry, and I am sure that much of this response resulted from her orphanage upbringing. She was born in an era where there was much less understanding of the emotional needs of children and undoubtedly this situation had profoundly affected her. My father was very overt with his emotions, but had some battles with mental health. I have spent my life trying to steer between these two extremes; not, I suspect, entirely successfully. There is a need for more research on the impact of family patterns, not least because more has been conducted with mothers than fathers.[5] It is not for nothing that the Bible recognises the significance of parenting: 'Start children off on the way they should go, and even when they are old they will not turn from it.'[6] We might surmise that the opposite is true – that when the start is poor the outlook can be, although not inevitably, bleak – and every counsellor will be aware of the enormous impact of our early years. Those of us who are parents will do much for our children (and grandchildren) if we can teach them both a vocabulary for their feelings and helpful ways to express them, and model that expression ourselves. I wish I had been able to do that better when my own children were growing up. I'm still trying with my grandchildren.

What about attitudes within the church to tears? It always makes me sad when someone says they cannot come to church because they might cry. I long for all churches to be places where people are welcomed, not just whatever they wear or look like, but whoever they are and however they come: in this context, to be places where it is safe to cry. We are inevitably impacted in church by our individual differences; we may not want to be seen crying, or fear we are thought to be attention-seeking. Yet we are encouraged to 'weep with those who weep'[7] – how can we do this as church together if the prevailing ethos is that tears are unwelcome, that the expectation is that Christians are always happy and victorious? In a peculiar irony, just as I started to type this paragraph, a CD which was playing on my computer began the song 'It Ain't No Sin to Get the Blues'.[8] One church I served in, at a particular stage in its history, excelled at vibrant praise worship. However, it struggled with finding a means of corporate expression when there were tragedies within the congregation. Churches need to learn to lament together in such times.[9] Another church was much more open about the reality of suffering, with both myself and my colleague often affirming that life can be tough, sometimes with tears in our own eyes, and including in worship both silence and songs which are more reflective and direct about wrestling with doubt, pain and faith. What we teach in our churches both in preaching and in liturgy and song choice is therefore key, as in every other aspect of our faith lives. We follow a suffering Lord who never promised us an easy time, only that he would be with us.[10]

There are several things which might bring us to tears in the spiritual life – such as gratitude for God's mercy or an appreciation of creation – and there are certainly times where because of natural factors (tiredness or life circumstances) we may be more prone to weeping in an atmosphere of worship. If we do not recognise the potential for tears in our faith journeys, and so suppress them, there is the risk of losing something which I think is very significant.

It is true, however, that even if we are generally free with our expression of emotion, there may be times when our tears will not come. As we noted earlier, in the early stages of grieving there is frequently a period of numbness where there may not be tears, particularly if the loss was a shock.[11] Depression, although sometimes resulting in tears which can be difficult to control, can also sometimes manifest instead with an inability to cry, linked with a general flatness in 'affect' – the word psychologists use for emotion.

Finally, if we become aware that we are carrying deep emotions but are unable to cry, are there any practical steps which might help? The place to start might be to work out if we are deliberately holding them in, and if so whether any of the factors above, or others, might be impacting on us. Do we need to subvert our own attitudes to our tears? Are there practical factors too, such as sheer busyness – and is that activity simply necessary, or are we using it to suppress what we feel? If we get to a point of recognising the need and desire to cry, the first step is often to find the right place, with enough time. Are we more comfortable to cry alone, or would it help to have a trusted friend with us? This is an important question, since if we have a history of holding tears in, we can have a deep-seated fear that if we start they will be uncontrollable. Also, if we have not in our family of origin known what it is like to cry and be comforted, we may either favour crying alone because it is familiar, or long for someone to see and honour our tears. It is not something to do five minutes before going into a meeting – we need to leave plenty of time to cry and then take some space to regain our equilibrium before whatever we need to do next. There is no right answer here: we are all different and will be helped in particular ways. If we live somewhere we don't want to be overheard, a private place is important – like a car, though of course it is important to find a safe place to park first. It might help to be outdoors; whatever is best for you. Then give space to think about what is making you sad (or angry, or whatever the emotion might be; sadness is not, as I have sought to demonstrate, the only emotion to find expression in tears). Simply let the emotion be, and don't feel you must cry – it just creates another pressure. If you do, that's OK, and if you don't, that's OK too; you have given yourself space to allow the feelings. If you do begin to weep, don't try to stop until you stop naturally.

I have often had to suppress sadness for quite valid reasons: for example, when conducting a funeral, where if we are leading the service it is important to 'hold' the emotions of others and keep our own in check to give space for those who are there. Similarly, in pastoral work, whilst it is unavoidable to be moved at times, and indeed it may help others to see we care, if we become too emotional, we will distract the person we are trying to help, as they become concerned about us. When I have had to keep my feelings at bay, I will often try to find a sad film to watch to give myself space to cry.

Sometimes our tears are unshed. But let's do all we can to let them be, seeing them as a gift from God.

Some questions to reflect on

- What was the attitude in your family of origin to crying, and what impact has it had?
- What seems to be the attitude to tears in any of the groups you are part of, including a church, if you attend one?
- Have there been any times in your life when you have been unable to cry? What might have been some of the reasons?
- What are some of the practical steps which might help you or others to allow tears when you or they need to?

14

Tears and Prayer

*In her deep anguish Hannah prayed to the
LORD, weeping bitterly.*[1]

A current story of tears and prayer

Sometimes we can become so hardened to the stories we see
and hear on the news. The sheer relentless number of reports
of death, pain and suffering can somehow blunt our capacity
to feel them any longer, as our hearts become hardened not by
disinterest but a combination of exhaustion and a pervading
sense of hopelessness.

Not that day. It began in an ordinary enough way, with a
simple family task. I was due to collect my daughter from university, about a three-hour drive in which I would have time to
think as I drove. I was looking forward to seeing her again and
having her home for a time.

Just before I left, I read a report online which changed that
journey completely. In many ways, sadly, it was not unusual.
Armed men had entered a Protestant church in the town of
Hantoukoura in Burkina Faso near the border with Niger,
killing the pastor and thirteen members of the congregation
including five teenagers, not much younger than my own

daughter.[2] This was not an isolated attack, but part of ongoing hostility against Christians. The organisation posting the account asked for prayer for those devastated by the loss of loved ones, and for strength and wisdom for the ongoing difficulty in living for Jesus in that area.

I set out on the journey, deciding to pray for that community as I drove. As I began to do so, however, tears which I simply could not control began to flow. They were quite different from the tears I have cried at other times when I have been distressed for myself or friends and family. They came from a very deep place, and I knew they were tears which expressed the deepest of prayers. As I focused on this group of people who I would never meet but who were my brothers and sisters because of our shared faith in Jesus, it was as though I connected with the heart of God, and his profound sorrow at the undeserved suffering of his children. I was separated by thousands of miles from them, but that distance was irrelevant. It was as though my spirit, held in God's love and his Spirit, could reach out in a way that was wordless but profound. I did not need to think out what I was praying, or give it words: in catching God's heart for them, my prayer went beyond words. The tears said more than my speaking ever could.

For some thirty minutes I prayed in this way, and then gently the tears dried and I resumed my journey. My task for that moment was done. I remained saddened, but at peace, and my journey continued towards my destination.

Reflecting on the Bible account: Hannah's story

No one really understood, and not everyone wanted to. Pain does that, doesn't it – some people do not want to come too close, think too deeply, for fear that somehow calamity is

contagious or they will find their helplessness in the face of it
unbearable. They want simply to be glad it is not them, becoming anxious as they realise it could be, just as easily. So, distance
from me may have created safety for them, but at the cost of
my increasing isolation from all those around me.

I was hopeful at first, of course. I saw so many women in
our village of Ramathaim, their bellies growing with, it seemed
to me, such ease. Some of them seemed to produce children so
effortlessly and regularly. Each time the village celebrated, I did
too, keeping to myself my sorrow at the sad comparison of my
empty womb. Yet with each new birth somehow the pain went
deeper as my hope diminished.

Then my husband took another wife. A younger woman.[3]
He loved me still, but could not understand how this action
of his only added to how unhappy and lost I felt, as the bar-
ren woman among so many, including now in my own household, who had sons and daughters. He tried to understand, and
when we would go as a family to Shiloh to sacrifice to God,
he would give me a double portion of the meat offering. He
wanted to make it right, I know that, but some things you can't
make right. You need to love, and go on loving, but in the way
that the person needs, not the way that makes you feel better.
Somehow, he would make my suffering about him, not me
and my distress. 'Don't I mean more to you than ten sons?'[4]
Well, no. It is not the same, dear husband. It is not about how
much I love you, not at all, and our love for each other, though
precious, did not ease my ache.

Peninnah did not understand either. She would hold her
children in front of me, just a few inches from my grasp. The
first time it happened I thought she was going to hand me the
baby to hold – that at least I could know how it felt to rest my
cheek on that baby hair, if even for a moment. But no. It was

a taunt. Year after year she produced children, not letting me share in their care but using them to underline the difference between our lives, jibing at me with her words. It was so cruel, yet perhaps she too was unhappy, watching each year the preferential treatment which was conferred on me.

Somehow it was especially difficult when we went to sacrifice and eat together. The excitement of the children, and the smell of incense and sacrifice in worship, and my husband well-meaning but thoughtless in giving me that double portion: a sign of blessing, when I felt anything but blessed. I could not understand why his God, who I worshipped too, had closed my womb. Each year as Peninnah privately mocked me I would weep until I had no stomach for the feast and my husband, gloriously oblivious with his quiver full of children, would ask me why.

And then one year it was different. The eating was over, and I was so tired of it all, so weary with my heart being broken by the loneliness of my plight. I stood to pray silently, not caring who saw, or what they thought, pouring out my heart to God, the tears my prayer. It was as if no one else was there, just me and God, as everything else faded. 'If only, God,' I begged inside, 'if only you will give me a son, he will be yours.'

No one understood, any more than they ever had. The family continued to celebrate, looking away in embarrassment at my show of emotion. I was swaying in my distress and mouthing unspoken words, but I did not care. I let the tears fall on the dust of the sanctuary by my feet. Every part of my heart flowed out in one last desperate prayer. After this, I decided, I would pray no more. I was done.

At first, I hardly noticed the priest drawing close, until he was stood beside me, his shadow alerting me to his presence. I was hoping for some word of comfort, some reassurance from this holy man that God had heard my prayer, that there was hope. Instead, his words, his accusation that I was drunk, only added to my sense of shame. I was unusually bold in my denial, though his words stung. I sensed then his regret at his hasty words as he gave me his blessing, and somehow my tears, the prayer and his eventual compassion brought me peace. For the first time in many festivals, I ate.

And before the next year was passed, there were tears of gratitude as I held my son. Samuel. 'God heard' – and he had.

(This part of Hannah's story comes from 1 Samuel 1:1 – 2:11.)

It seems to me that the relationship between tears and prayer is a complex one, and I certainly will not have the last word here. I hope, as we near the end of our journey together, that you are more able to welcome your tears, of all kinds, as an important part of our emotional life, and as a gift from God, in all their varied forms. As such, they are therefore to be celebrated as part of our faith journey.

If that is the case, it is not surprising that at times when bringing our concerns to God tears may be an integral and important part of our prayer life. Knowing I was writing this book, someone made contact with me to relate a story illustrating exactly that. A single mother, she was approaching the time when her son, who had additional needs, would be leaving home for further study. Like many parents, she found this deeply sad, grieving ahead of his leaving home, for all that it would mean, both for him and for her.

She spent ten consecutive days crying and the only thing she could do was ask God to help. Her friends were wonderfully kind and supportive, but nothing they said helped the tears to stop flowing. Praying and asking God for peace and hope for his future was all she could do. She decided to fast and pray, and felt God reminded her of how many times he had healed her broken and battered heart, and showed her that, as well as being a mother, she was much more than that and there were adventures ahead for her. Just writing the story to send to me brought her more tears, but she – rightly, I think – accepted that it was OK to cry, that God saw all of her tears and kept them safe. As she expressed it: 'Praying does not always stop the tears, but it starts a conversation with God. My tears connect me to the one who loves me and the one who loves my son, and after crying and praying I know that all will be well.'

I have at times experienced that same peace after crying in prayer to God during times of distress, but in all honesty, not always. I suspect that at those times I have used prayer to shut down my tears for fear that I might not be able to stop. I recognise that I need instead to be patient with my tearful prayers and give them all the time they need rather than rushing on or pushing them away.

Just as there are many kinds of tears, there are many kinds of prayer. Teaching on prayer often uses the acronym A.C.T.S. – adoration, confession, thanks and supplication, or alternatively thanks, sorry, please – tsp., the shortened version of teaspoon used in recipes. Tears, it seems to me, can be a part of any of those forms of prayer. I have sometimes, for example, found tears in my eyes looking at something beautiful in creation. Some years ago, I had the immense privilege of visiting Iceland. Because it is so sparsely populated, there are many places where you can see nothing except the beauty of the land – an extraordinary place which a friend described as 'creation in the making'. It is a country where glaciers meet green areas, volcanoes rise out of lava fields and steam bursts from multicoloured rocks. Stopping at one place, where snowy peaks could be seen at the far side of a vast lake, the sheer beauty of it elicited from me a prayer of thanks expressed mainly in wordless tears. I find that I am often moved to tears in worship (and sometimes in preaching), most frequently as I realise afresh the enormity of God's love.

However, my experience is that tears in prayer happen most when we are praying for others and can't find the words as we touch just a little of God's far greater heart. I have certainly experienced crying during prayer of this kind, which has felt very different from simple human concern. One friend described how in prayer for young men in a football team he had a connection with, his deep longing to see them come to faith and see their lives changed as his had been flowed in tears. On one occasion I was at a meeting where we were in prayer for the community. As we prayed, I was reminded of a picture I had received, some years before but also in prayer, of a birds' eye view of rows of houses. In the image I could see that the people inside were naked and unprotected, completely vulnerable to the elements, which I interpreted as spiritual rather than physical. As I shared it with the meeting I began to weep with compassion. It was not sobbing, and my face did not contort – tears simply flowed from my eyes. It was not personal distress, or even empathy: the feeling was completely different. I have experienced something similar on several occasions and spoken to others who have said that intermittently they have also experienced tears of a completely different kind in this way. It would appear that perhaps the source is different; a specific gift of the Spirit for this occasion rather than human emotion, which is also given by God but is there within us at all times. Tears shed in this way seem to simply flow without any of the other physical signs associated with crying, such as facial movements.

Richard Foster, in his book on prayer,[5] writes about 'the prayer of tears'. He particularly explores the place of tears in prayer in the context of weeping for our sin and the sin of God's people, rather like the description in Ezra: 'While Ezra was praying and confessing, weeping and throwing himself down before the house of God, a large crowd of Israelites – men, women and children – gathered round him. They too wept bitterly.'[6] He points out that church tradition sees this godly sorrow as a good thing, a sign of closeness to God and in fact linked with joy.[7] This was much more openly spoken and written about in the early church, particularly in the writings of the desert fathers and mothers from the fourth to sixth centuries. It was accepted that at times people would have an experience of God which overflowed in tears, as a way of cleansing the soul and laying down our pride. I suspect allowing this gift of repentant tears to lead us to joy is harder than it sounds. There have certainly been times when, having messed up particularly badly, I have cried over it in prayer as I have brought it to God. However, I can find it difficult to not continue to wallow in self-criticism and instead genuinely receive, after the tears, a resulting peace. To understand grace and forgiveness in the heart as well as the head is an important challenge.

Like other charismatic gifts (such as speaking in tongues), the gift of tears was seen by the desert mothers and fathers as an endowment coming entirely from God's grace, and could be received once, several times, or throughout a person's life. Although the gift of tears is not mentioned in the Bible in the lists of charismatic gifts,[8] the New Testament lists are different from one another and there is nothing to suggest that even together they are a full and exhaustive list. As with any gift of the Spirit, they do not indicate superiority on our part (they are gift, not reward) and the focus should remain on the Giver rather than develop into an excessive preoccupation with whether we do or do not receive a particular gift. Perhaps too we will never disentangle the human elements from the work of God and do not need to do so.

At other times, it seems to me, the tears *are* the prayer, particularly when we simply cannot find the words. In 2 Kings 20, King Hezekiah becomes ill. As he prays and weeps, the two things seem inextricably linked, and God hears both as if they are one: 'I have heard your prayer and seen your tears'.[9] Hannah's tears, so clearly misunderstood by Eli, were a wordless prayer from the heart expressed in her weeping. Prayer of any kind can also be expressed in these wordless tears.

This is an area, I suspect, which needs to be explored and researched a good deal more. Tears can be a vital part of the great privilege of prayer, and one of the many ways to grow in our relationship with God.

Some questions to reflect on

- Have you had any times when your tears have been a part or all of a prayer?
- Do you see tears as a spiritual gift?
- Have you experienced times when you have felt your tears to be of a different kind? What were the circumstances?
- Think about or read about some of the different kinds of prayer. Have you experienced tears with any of the different kinds?

15

The Ending of Tears

And I heard a loud voice from the throne saying,
'Look! God's dwelling-place is now among the
people, and he will dwell with them. They will
be his people, and God himself will be with
them and be their God. "He will wipe every tear
from their eyes. There will be no more death" or
mourning or crying or pain, for the old order of
things has passed away.'[1]

I thought long and hard about the structure of this chapter, and you will have noticed (unless you started here) that it follows a different pattern. If I had retained the same shape, this section would have been a current story, followed by an imaginative retelling of a biblical story, and then some general reflection.

Actually, this chapter does not even have the same title that it started with. It began life as 'The Healing of Tears', and at that stage I was already wrestling with whether to keep the same structure as the other chapters, or to change it. It was clear to me that I wanted the final chapter to feature this passage from Revelation, not least because it is the last reference in the Bible to tears. I felt instinctively, though, that somehow it needed to be treated differently.

As I continued to reflect, I realised I was unhappy with the chapter title itself. I'm not sure that tears need healing – rather, they themselves can be, at times, therapeutic. Jean Gakwandi writes movingly of creating places and times to weep for widows in the aftermath of the 1994 genocide in Rwanda.[2] I say at times because, in all honesty, sometimes shedding tears have left me feeling no better, though I accept in theory that the physical release is helpful at some level. At other times, however, they have helped enormously and been restorative and one of the ways that healing has come. It depends on a huge number of factors for me as to how therapeutic they have felt – for example, the reason for them, if they have felt held by God and/or others, and if I have felt obliged to choke them down for some reason, rather than let them flow.

The entire premise of this book is that our tears are God-given, part of our humanity. Like the full range of emotions we experience as people, I believe they are to be welcomed as friends rather than feared and repressed. What needs healing is not the tears but the wounds from the hurt and grief we experience which cause us to weep. Other circumstances we have covered in this book which result in tears – friendship, gratitude and so on – most certainly do not need healing, but rather embracing and celebrating, though perhaps even these will become subsumed in the completely new future life of which Revelation speaks. There is much mystery that we do not understand. So, the chapter title was changed to its current more accurate reflection of the biblical passage above.

My other difficulty was that I have wanted to be real in this book, and this text – which I will look at shortly – describes an ending of tears which is yet to come. It assumes that tears caused by loss and all other painful experiences will finish. It seems to me that tears will never fully end in the life we experience now – not until the future time envisaged in the final two chapters of Revelation when everything is restored to God's original plan, or perhaps more accurately, a new one comes to fruition. Some readers may disagree with me, citing stories of deep, perhaps even immediate, release from pain and tears caused by huge traumas. However, that has not been my experience. With smaller hurts, like a scratch where the skin is fully restored, the tears have done their work and healing is complete. With deeper sources of pain, however, at times I have felt God's gentle presence, a balm, but the tears, including but not confined to those I have shared in this book, still return at times. They may have been eased, but have not ended. The experiences which lie beneath them, stretching across the years, have made me the woman I am today, and sit at the very foundation of who I am. On occasions tears flow because situations in the present mirror those from the past. In fact, in contrast to tears diminishing, at times they are cumulative. Like us all, I carry scars which sometimes weep rather than bleed. So, I feel I cannot write with integrity about something this personal when it is outside my experience. If the ending of tears in the present is part of your story, I am glad.

So, what about this future promise? Revelation is a curious book, often avoided, at least in large sections, both by individuals and churches. It is certainly difficult in places in its imagery, some of it unfamiliar, some of it richly biblical. It is worth studying and unpacking, but that is not the purpose here. It was written in the late first century and no doubt the earliest readers understood the symbolic language in its immediate cultural context with greater ease. Yet the themes it addresses – the worship of other things apart from God, the tyranny of political systems and the cost of discipleship – are as real now as they were then. The writer's ultimate vision of the restoration of creation and the final triumph of God is a sublime theme, finding its climax in the beautiful words in the section above and throughout the final two chapters.

It does not take any imagination to see the brokenness of our world – watching the news is enough. It takes rather more to hold on to the hope that this is not all there is, that there will come a time when the cosmic sources of chaos and destruction (which the 'sea' represents in Revelation[3]) are finally overcome. This is the hope the writer offers us, describing a reality where everything will be new, not just a cleaned-up version of what we experience now, but rather something where the very essence is transformed. It is a vision that shows the present order for the meaningless sham it really is. Instead, this is a totally new existence, where God is so present, so completely and eternally 'Immanuel',[4] that darkness is dispelled,[5] and there is no possibility of '"death" or mourning or crying or pain'.[6] What is often humankind's greatest source of pain, the separation of death, is finally defeated and there is the ultimate fulfilment of the promise that 'those who mourn . . . will be comforted'.[7] It is a rout which the death and resurrection of Jesus signalled, but which will find its completion in the future promised here. It does not suggest for us, as is often portrayed, some form of floating spirit-only existence. In contrast, the earth is transformed as heaven and earth are united in the full presence of God, the two becoming so intrinsically linked that the values and reality of heaven transform earth so that the two are indistinguishable. They were once joined in the person of Jesus, now they are united fully, completely and eternally.

Earlier in Revelation the writer describes his tears shed because no one could open the scroll to reveal what was ahead:[8] there his weeping stopped at the realisation of the presence of the Lamb, Jesus. Now the need for all tears has gone. The 'groaning'[9] is ended. The Lamb has triumphed. An unassailable answer has been given to the world's evil. God is fully with his people, as was promised[10] and longed for throughout history. It makes me want to shout a heartfelt: 'At last! Yes!'

The picture here is beautifully tender – God wiping away the tears himself.[11] On occasions I have done that for others, gently making that intimate gesture as I held them when words have failed. Here God does so, drawing as close to his creation as it is possible to get. The monumental struggle with the foul reality of evil – seen through the whole Bible story from the dawn of creation, through the demonic battles played out in the life of Jesus, to this final culmination as everything is renewed – is finally over. It is a wrestling which is still an all too familiar reality, as I write, in the life of people of faith and in all of humanity. The day will come, though, this passage reminds us, when it will be in the past, with only a glorious future to come.

Some final questions to reflect on

- Have there been any times in your life when you have experienced the healing of God, physically, emotionally, or spiritually?
- As we come towards the end of this book, have you learned any new things about your own tears? Can you take the opportunity to write them down, or share with a friend or discussion group?
- Might there be someone God is calling you to wipe away tears from now, in the present?
- What difference might it make to you to hold onto the hope for the future described by the writer of Revelation?

Final Reflections

So, we have reached the end of our journey together. I do hope that whether you have read it alone or with others in a group, you have learned some new things, but also to value a little more the full range of emotions that we have as people. It is so important to accept the emotions we experience and try to understand them rather than view them with fear or hostility and so try to suppress them. This is a brave, but crucial, start to better understanding ourselves.

I hope that in particular you have become a little more appreciative of your tears, in whatever circumstances they are cried. They are God-given and if Jesus could weep then it has to be possible and right for us to do so too, however much some of us fear the vulnerability that it brings. I am still on that journey myself.

You may have found some chapters easier than others. I would encourage you to come back another time to any you might have skimmed or skipped altogether, and gently ask yourself why they might be especially daunting. If it would help, there are some resources at the end of the book as a start-ing place for help with some of the issues raised, or you might want to seek out a trusted friend, or other kinds of help. Sharing our story with another is a sign of great strength and courage.

I would love to hear from you if you have comments to make or stories to share, and I can be contacted via www.jeanniekendall.co.uk.

Above all, I hope this book will help you to be kinder towards others and yourself at times of tears: to know that they are precious to God and that he holds them in that bottle because he has seen and treasures each one. He loves you more than you can possibly imagine.

Acknowledgements

It is my name on the cover of this book, but I owe so much to so many people for bringing it to birth.

I'm indebted again to the fantastic team at Authentic, Donna, Becky, Rachael, Charlie and my editor for this book, Sheila Jacobs. They are an absolute joy to work with and a constant source of encouragement. I can't think of better midwives for this second 'baby'.

My profound thanks go to Adrian Plass for agreeing to write the Foreword. His words of encouragement about my writing decades ago led me to persist, and his books over the years, in particular their honesty, have had a profound influence on my life. I have laughed and cried at them, and been equally glad of both. Along with the Narnia books, they are my go-to place in desert times.

Those who took the time to read and endorse this book – I am really grateful to you for carving out time in your busy lives.

The staff and congregation at Streatham Baptist Church, especially Dave Lock at Manna Christian Centre, and the church family and staff, in particular Phil, at Beeches Baptist Church – you all have a place in my heart and always will, and have been such an encouragement on this writing journey.

My special thanks to Rachel Johnson for again checking the earliest version, and even more for five decades of friendship.

My thanks to Steff Wright for minimising my stress by rescuing me with some formatting issues.

Thank you again to all of you who have shared your stories – I do so hope you are pleased with the results. Thank you for your openness and trust.

Thank you to all of you who bought or read the first book, came to various speaking engagements and encouraged me along the way.

To those few friends over the years who I have allowed to see my tears – thank you for allowing me to be vulnerable: you know how hard I find it!

Most of all, my heart belongs to my precious family – to Malc, my companion of four decades and my biggest supporter. Your love for me is so constant. To my children, Amy and Ross, and their spouses, Vali and Helen: I hope you know how much I love you. And my precious grandchildren, Faith and Gabriel: I hope in time you will read this book, and even more, I hope that you will discover Jesus for yourselves. I love you all more than my words, or my tears, can express.

Above all, none of this would have been possible without my friendship with you, Jesus. I've let you down so many times, but you have seen every tear and held them in your biggest of bottles. I owe you everything, and I only hope this book draws those who read it a little closer to you.

Bibliography

Asher, Jane and Gerald Scarfe, *Moppy is Angry* (Trowbridge: Positive Press, 2004).

Atkinson, David J., David H. Field, Arthur F. Holmes, and Oliver O'Donovan (ed.), *New Dictionary of Christian Ethics and Pastoral Theology* (Downers Grove, IL: InterVarsity Press, 1995).

Barclay, William, *The Daily Study Bible: Revelation of John, Volume 2* (Edinburgh: The Saint Andrew Press, 1960 ed.).

Barclay, William, *The Daily Study Bible: The Letters to the Corinthians* (Edinburgh: The Saint Andrew Press, 1975 ed.).

Barclay, William, *The Daily Study Bible: The Letters of James and Peter* (Edinburgh: The Saint Andrew Press, 1976 ed.).

Berne, Eric, *Games People Play: The Psychology of Human Relationships* (New York: Ballantine Books, 1964).

Bowlby, John, *Attachment* (London: Random House, 1997).

Bowlby, John, *A Secure Base* (Abingdon: Routledge, 2005).

Bristow, John, *What Paul Really Said About Women* (New York: HarperCollins, 1991).

Brown, Brené, *I Thought It Was Just Me (But it isn't)* (New York: J.P. Tarcher/Penguin Putnam, 2008).

Brown, Brené, *Daring Greatly* (New York: Gotham Books, 2012).

Brown, Brené, *The Gifts of Imperfection* (Center City, MN: Hazelden Publishing, 2018).

Brueggemann, Walter, *Interpretation: A Bible Commentary for Preaching and Teaching: Genesis* (Atlanta, GA: John Knox Press, 1982).

Caird, G.B., *The Revelation of St John the Divine* (London: A & C Black, 1966).

Coate, Mary Anne, *Clergy Stress* (London: SPCK, 1989).

Collins-Donnelly, Kate, *Starving the Stress Gremlin* (London: Jessica Kingsley Publications, 2013).

Colwell, John E., *Why Have You Forsaken Me? A Personal Reflection on the Experience of Desolation* (Milton Keynes: Paternoster, 2009).

Dahl, Roald, *The BFG* (London: Jonathan Cape, 1982).

Dixon, Thomas, *Weeping Britannia: Portrait of a Nation in Tears* (Oxford: Oxford University Press, 2015).

Dormandy, Richard, *Shabby Treasure* (Pimlico: Brindley Books, 2006).

Dormandy, Richard, *The Madness of St Paul* (Chawton: Redemptorist Publications, 2011).

Erikson, Erik, *Childhood and Society* (New York: W.W. Norton & Co., 1950 ed.).

Erikson, Erik, *Identity and the Life Cycle* (New York: W.W. Norton & Co., 1980 ed.).

Foster, Richard, *Prayer* (London: Hodder & Stoughton, 1992).

Frey, William H. II, Ann Lauterbach, Rose-Lynn Fisher, *The Topography of Tears* (New York: Bellevue Literary Press, 2017).

Gaarder, Jostein, *The Christmas Mystery* (London: Phoenix House, 1996).

Gaebelein, Frank E. (ed.), *The Expositor's Bible Commentary, Volume 2: Genesis to Numbers* (Grand Rapids, MI: Zondervan, 1990).

Gakwandi, Jean with Karin Heidrich, *Solace: The Story of Solace Ministries* (Kigali: Solace Ministries, 2015).

Goldingay, John, *After Eating the Apricot* (Cumbria: Paternoster, 1996).

Goldingay, John, *Walk On: Life, Loss, Trust, and Other Realities* (Grand Rapids, MI: Baker Academic, 2002).

Goldingay, John, *Genesis for Everyone, Part 1* (London: SPCK, 2010).

Goldingay, John, *Genesis for Everyone, Part 2* (London: SPCK, 2010).

Goldingay, John, *Joshua, Judges & Ruth for Everyone* (London: SPCK, 2011).

Goldingay, John, *1 & 2 Samuel for Everyone* (London: SPCK, 2011).

Holmes, Jeremy, *John Bowlby and Attachment Theory* (Makers of Modern Psychotherapy) (Abingdon: Routledge, 2014).

Hurding, Roger F., *Roots & Shoots: A Guide to Counselling and Psychotherapy* (London: Hodder & Stoughton, 2003 ed.).

Jacobs, Michael, *Swift to Hear* (London: SPCK, 1985).

Jacobs, Michael, *The Presenting Past* (Maidenhead: Open University Press, 2012 ed.).

Johnson, Alan F., *The Expositor's Bible Commentary: Revelation* (Grand Rapids, MI: Zondervan, 1996).

Jones, Nigel A., *Samuel, the Boy: Life Lessons from the First Four Chapters of 1 Samuel* (Bloomington, IN: Westbow Press, 2019).

Keating, Thomas, *Invitation to Love: The Way of Christian Contemplation* (London: Bloomsbury, 2012 ed.).

Kendall, Jeannie, *Finding Our Voice* (Milton Keynes: Authentic Media, 2019).

Kidner, Derek, *Genesis: An Introduction and Commentary* (London: The Tyndale Press, 1967).

Lendrum, Susan and Gabrielle Syme, *Gift of Tears: A Practical Approach to Loss and Bereavement in Counselling and Psychotherapy* (Abingdon: Routledge, 2004 ed.).

Littledale, Richard, *Postcards from the Land of Grief* (Milton Keynes: Authentic Media, 2019).

Maslow, Abraham H., *A Theory of Human Motivation* (Radford, VA: Wilder Publications, 2013).

Mearns, P., & B. Thorne, *Person-Centred Counselling in Action* (Counselling in Action series) (London: SAGE Publications Ltd., 2013 ed.).

Millar, Roy, *Come and See: An Invitation to Journey with Jesus and His Beloved Disciple John* (Watford: Instant Apostle, 2019).

Milne, A.A., *Winnie-the-Pooh: The Complete Collection of Stories and Poems: Hardback Slipcase Volume (Winnie-the-Pooh – Classic Editions)* (London: Egmont, 2016).

Morris, Leon, *Revelation: An Introduction and Commentary* (London: The Tyndale Press, 1969).

Morris, Leon, *The Gospel According to John* (London: Marshall, Morgan & Scott, 1971).

Murray Parkes, Colin, *Bereavement: Studies of Grief in Adult Life* (London: Penguin, 2010 ed.).

Musters, Claire, *Taking Off the Mask* (Milton Keynes: Authentic Media, 2017).

Nouwen, Henri, *The Return of the Prodigal Son* (London: Darton, Longman & Todd, 1994 ed.).

Oliver, Stephen (ed.), *Inside Grief* (London: SPCK, 2013).

Percey, Andy, *Infused with Life* (Milton Keynes: Authentic Media, 2019).

Peterson, Eugene H., *The Message of David* (London: Marshall Pickering, 1997).

Pytches, Mary, *Who Am I? Discovering Your Identity in Christ* (London: Hodder & Stoughton, 1999).

Richardson, Jan, *The Cure for Sorrow* (Orlando, FL: Wanton Gospeller Press, 2016).

Rogers, Carl, *Client-Centered Therapy: Its Current Practice, Implications and Theory* (London: Constable, 1951).

Rowley, H.H., *Job* (London: Thomas Nelson & Sons, 1970).

Rowling, J.K., *Harry Potter and the Philosopher's Stone* (London: Bloomsbury Publishing, 1997).

Runcorn, David, *Rumours of Life: Transforming Wounded People* (London: SPCK, 2006).

Runcorn, David, *The Language of Tears* (Norwich: Canterbury Press, 2018).

Saunders, Cicely, *Beyond the Horizon* (London: Darton, Longman & Todd, 1990).

Smick, Elmer B., *The Expositor's Bible Commentary Volume 4: Job* (Grand Rapids, MI: Zondervan, 1988).

Stott, John, *The Message of Acts* (Leicester: Inter-Varsity Press, 1990).

Tenney, Merrill C., *The Expositor's Bible Commentary: John* (Grand Rapids, MI: Zondervan, 1995).

Tenney, Merrill C., *Interpreting Revelation* (Grand Rapids, MI: Eerdmans Publishing Company, 1957).

Trible, Phyllis, *Texts of Terror* (London: SCM, 2002).

Trible, Phyllis and Letty M. Russell (ed.), *Hagar, Sarah and Their Children* (Louisville, KY: Westminster John Knox Press, 2006).

Wallin, David J., *Attachment in Psychotherapy* (New York: Guilford Press, 2007).

Watt Smith, Tiffany, *The Book of Human Emotions* (London: Wellcome Collection, 2016).

White, E.B., *Charlotte's Web* (New York: Harper & Brothers, 1952).

Wilcock, Michael, *The Message of Revelation* (London: Inter-Varsity Press, 1975).

Witherington III, Ben, *Revelation* (Cambridge: Cambridge University Press, 2003).

Worden, William J., *Grief Counselling and Grief Therapy* (London: Tavistock/Routledge, 1983).

Worden, William J., *Grief Counselling and Grief Therapy: A Handbook for the Mental Health Practitioner* (Abingdon: Routledge, 2010 ed.).

Wright, Tom, *John for Everyone, Part 2, Chapters 11–21* (London: SPCK, 2002).

Wright, Tom, *Revelation for Everyone* (London: SPCK, 2011).

Yancey, Philip, *Where is God When it Hurts?* (Grand Rapids, MI: Zondervan, 2002 ed.).

Yancey, Philip, *The Question That Never Goes Away: What is God Up To in a World of Such Tragedy and Pain?* (London: Hodder & Stoughton, 2013).

Journals and Articles

Ariely, D., E. Kamenica and D. Prelec, 'Man's search for meaning: The Case of Legos', *Journal of Economic Behavior & Organization*, 67 (3–4): pp. 671–77 (2008).

Beike, D.R., K.D. Markman and F. Karadogan, 'Lost Opportunities: A Theory of Regret Intensity', *Personality and Social Psychology Bulletin*, 35: pp. 385–97 (2009).

Newall, N.E., J.G. Chipperfield, L.M. Daniels, S. Hladkyj, and R.P. Perry, 'Regret in Later Life: Exploring Relationships Between Regret Frequency, Secondary Interpretive Control Beliefs, and Health in Older Individuals', *International Journal of Aging and Human Development*, 68: pp. 261–88 (2009).

Norcross, J.C., B.E. Zimmerman, R.P. Greenberg and J.K. Swift, 'Do All Therapists Do That When Saying Goodbye? A Study of Commonalities in Termination Behaviors', American Psychological Association publication *Psychotherapy*, Vol. 54, No. 1: pp. 66–7 (2017). https://www.newstatesman.com/culture/books/2016/01/stiff-upper-lips-english-history-emotion (accessed 26 September 2020).

https://www.psychologytoday.com/us/blog/living-the-questions/201401/how-crack-the-code-men-s-feelings (accessed 26 September 2020).

https://www.researchgate.net/publication/314269329_Do_all_therapists_do_that_when_saying_goodbye_A_study_of_commonalities_in_termination_behaviors

https://www.thelancet.com/journals/lancet/article/PIIS0140-6736(14)60093-3/fulltext (accessed 26 September 2020).

Websites

General and biblical

https://www.smithsonianmag.com/science-nature/the-microscopic-structures-of-dried-human-tears-180947766/ (accessed 1 August 2019).

https://www.psychologytoday.com (accessed 10 August 2019).

https://www.christianitytoday.com/ct/topics/p/prosperity-gospel/ (accessed 10 August 2019).

https://www.eauk.org/assets/files/downloads/Reviewing-the-discourse-of-Spiritual-Abuse.pdf (accessed 10 August 2019).

https://www.simplypsychology.org/maslow.html#targetText=Maslow's%20hierarchy%20of%20needs%20is,hierarchical%20levels%20within%20a%20pyramid.&targetText=From%20the%20bottom%20of%20the,%2C%20esteem%20and%20self-actualization (accessed 31 October 2019).

https://kidshelpline.com.au/parents/issues/helping-kids-identify-and-express-feelings (accessed 2 November 2019).

http://www.jewishencyclopedia.com/articles/1944-ashes (accessed 24 December 2019).

https://www.myjewishlearning.com/article/timeline-of-jewish-mourning/ (accessed 24 December 2019).

https://spiritualdirection.com/2015/01/26/what-is-the-gift-of-tears (accessed 14 January 2020).

Regret

https://psychology.iresearchnet.com/social-psychology/emotions/regret/ (accessed 25 November 2019).

Family

https://www.psychologytoday.com/intl/articles/199301/adult-sibling-rivalry (accessed 1 October 2019).

https://scholarworks.gvsu.edu/cgi/viewcontent.cgi?article=1061&context=orpc (accessed 1 October 2019).

Friendship and relationships

https://www.psychologytoday.com/gb/blog/brain-waves/201703/the-three-basics-friendship (accessed 14 August 2019).

https://www.medicalnewstoday.com/articles/319873.php (accessed 3 January 2020).

Loss

https://www.scienceandnonduality.com/article/the-geography-of-sorrow?fbclid=IwAR2oR2lt1pGLHf7-Oi4MID_otF4RSQpCxqmd8K4V_CZMeOEoOK1JDI9gUSc (accessed 23 December 2019).

https://www.researchgate.net/publication/314269329_Do_all_ therapists_do_that_when_saying_goodbye_A_study_of_ commonalities_in_termination_behaviors (accessed 6 January 2020).

Anger

https://www.newscientist.com/article/mg21729032-700-do-get-mad-the-upside-of-anger/ (accessed 14 September 2019).

https://www.nhs.uk/conditions/stress-anxiety-depression/ about-anger/ (accessed 14 September 2019).

Stress

https://www.nhsinform.scot/healthy-living/mental-wellbeing/ stress/struggling-with-stress (accessed 21 October 2019).

https://www.mentalhealth.org.uk/a-to-z/s/stress (accessed 21 October 2019).

https://www.stress.org/about/hans-selye-birth-of-stress (accessed 21 October 2019).

https://www.stress.org/holmes-rahe-stress-inventory (accessed 21 October 2019).

https://www.nhs.uk/conditions/cognitive-behavioural-therapy-cbt/ (accessed 21 October 2019).

Organisations Offering Support and Information

All details correct at the time of publication, but may be subject to change

GENERAL

APSE: For information about people and organisations involved in pastoral supervision, including lists of pastoral supervisors. Visit: https://www.pastoralsupervision.org.uk/

British Association for Counselling and therapy: https://www.bacp.co.uk/ to find lists of individuals offering support and counselling near where you live and other counselling-related information.

Care for the Family: Support and training on a range of issues. Visit: https://www.careforthefamily.org.uk/

Premier Lifeline: Listening service from a Christian perspective. Phone: 0300 111 0101.

MENTAL HEALTH ISSUES

Breathing Space: Offers a confidential phone and web-based support for people in Scotland. Phone: 0800 83 85 87. Visit: https://breathingspace.scot/

CALM: (the Campaign Against Living Miserably) aims to prevent male suicide in the UK and offers anonymous, confidential listening and information. Phone: 0800 58 58 58. Visit: https://www.thecalmzone.net/

Community Advice & Listening Line: Offers emotional support and information on mental health for people in Wales. Phone: 0800 132 737 or text 'help' to 81066. Visit: http://www.callhelpline.org.uk/

HOPELineUK: Offers support, practical advice and information to young people considering suicide and for others who are concerned for someone. Phone: 0800 068 41 41. Visit: https://papyrus-uk.org/

Lifeline: provides support to people in Northern Ireland, regardless of age or district. Phone: 0808 808 8000. Visit: https://www.lifelinehelpline.info/

Mind: Provides advice and support for anyone experiencing a mental health issue. For information email info@mind.org.uk. Phone: 0300 123 3393; text: 86463. Visit: https://www.mind.org.uk/

Nightlines: Confidential support services run by students for students. Visit: https://www.nightline.ac.uk/want-to-talk/

Shout: A 24/7 text service, free on most mobile networks, for anyone struggling to cope and in need of immediate help. Text SHOUT to 85258. Visit: https://www.giveusashout.org/get-help/

The Samaritans: Help twenty-four hours a day for anyone struggling to cope, providing a safe place to talk. Phone: 116 123; email: jo@samaritans.org. Visit: https://www.samaritans.org/

ADDICTIONS

Al-Anon: Help for friends and families of alcoholics. Helpline: 0800 0086 811 or email via https://www.al-anonuk.org.uk/

Alcoholics Anonymous: Helpline: 0800 9177650 or to locate a meeting: https://www.alcoholics-anonymous.org.uk/

Gamblers Anonymous: Information line: 0330 094 0322 or email info@gamblersanonymous.org.uk; visit: https://www.gamblersanonymous.org.uk

Overeaters Anonymous: Phone 07798 587802; worldwide: https://oa.org/ UK: https://www.oagb.org.uk/

PHOBIAS

Anxiety UK: https://www.anxietyuk.org.uk/anxiety-type/phobias/

Mind: https://www.mind.org.uk/information-support/types-of-mental-health-problems/phobias/

The NHS: https://www.nhsinform.scot/healthy-living/mental-wellbeing/fears-and-phobias/help-for-phobias

AFTER A LOSS

Cruse Bereavement Care: Face-to-face, telephone, email and website support. Helpline: 0808 808 1677. Visit: https://www.cruse.org.uk/

Sands: Support following the stillbirth or neonatal death of a baby. Helpline: 0808 164 3332 (free from a landline) or email helpline@sands.org.uk. Visit: https://www.sands.org.uk/

SLOW: For a list of organisations offering support after a bereavement. Visit: https://slowgroup.co.uk/uk-bereavement-support-organisations/

Survivors of Bereavement by Suicide: For those bereaved by the suicide of a close relative or friend. Phone: 0300 111 5065. Visit: https://uksobs.org/

The Compassionate Friends: Offering support after the death of a child at any age. UK National Helpline: 0345 123 2304; email helpline@tcf.org.uk. Visit: https://www.tcf.org.uk/

HEALTH INFORMATION

NHS sites: Various links can be found on https://www.nhs.uk

RELATIONSHIP SUPPORT

Carers UK: Support for carers. Visit: https://www.carersuk.org/Home

Relate: Offers advice and relationship counselling, workshops, mediation, consultations and support. Phone: 0300 100 1234. Visit: https://www.relate.org.uk/

Notes

Foreword

[1] This translation is from the original NIV, © International Bible Society, first published in Great Britain in 1979. The NIV was revised in 1984 and 2011 and so this verse now reads differently.

Introduction

[1] Jeannie Kendall, *Finding Our Voice* (Milton Keynes: Authentic, 2019).

[2] See https://www.smithsonianmag.com/science-nature/the-microscopic-structures-of-dried-human-tears-180947766/ (accessed 19 September 2020).

[3] See https://www.nationalgeographic.com/news/2015/07/150714-animal-dog-thinking-feelings-brain-science/.

[4] See https://www.sciencefocus.com/the-human-body/are-we-the-only-animals-that-cry/ (accessed 19 September 2020).

[5] Rom. 8:26.

[6] John Goldingay, *Walk On: Life, Loss, Trust, and Other Realities* (Grand Rapids, MI: Baker Academic, 2002), p. 160.

[7] Ps. 139:14.

1 Tears of Regret

[1] Heb. 12:16,17.

[2] See https://psychology.iresearchnet.com/social-psychology/emotions/regret/ (accessed 19 September 2020).

[3] See for example https://qz.com/work/1298110/a-new-study-on-the-psychology-of-persistent-regrets-can-teach-you-how-to-live-now/ (accessed 19 September 2020).

[4] See Neal J. Roese, Ginger L. Pennington, Jill Coleman, Maria Janicki, Norman P. Li, and Douglas T. Kenrick, https://www.ncbi.nlm.nih.gov/pmc/articles/PMC2293329/#:~:targetText=Of%20the%20various%20ratings%20of,missing%20an%20opportunity%20for%20sex (accessed 19 September 2020).

[5] See Melanie Greenberg https://www.psychologytoday.com/gb/blog/the-mindful-self-express/201206/the-neuroscience-regret (accessed 19 September 2020).

[6] Gen. 27:41.

[7] The story is recorded in Gen. 33.

[8] See for example Luke 22:1–3,47,48.

[9] Luke 22:54–62.

[10] Matt. 27:3–5.

[11] 1 Cor. 15:5.

[12] John 21:15–19.

2 Tears of Family Pain

[1] Gen. 37:35.

[2] Gen. 33:4.

[3] Gen. 43:30; 45:2,14,15; 46:29; 50:1,17.

[4] Gen. 45:14.

[5] See Gen. 29:18–30.

[6] These were their names initially in the story, later changed to Abraham – meaning 'father of many' – and Sarah in Gen. 17.

[7] 2 Sam. 13:7–14, see Phyllis Trible, *Texts of Terror* (London: SCM Press, 2002), pp. 25–44. There are examples of biblical marriages

between relatives, such as, it would seem, Abraham and Sarah (Gen. 20:12) and Isaac and Rebekah (Gen. 24:3,4) but in the early stages of human history this was not unusual. The Law of Moses, the Torah, which forms the basis for Old Testament morality, came later.

[8] 1 Sam. 30, 2 Sam. 12 and 2 Sam. 18.

[9] See 1 Sam. 2:12 in relation to Eli's sons.

[10] William Barclay, *The Daily Study Bible: The Letters of James and Peter* (Edinburgh: The Saint Andrew Press, 1976 ed.), p. 210.

[11] https://www.pbs.org/empires/romans/empire/family.html (accessed 19 September 2020).

[12] See James Georgas, 'Family: Variations and Changes Across Cultures', https://scholarworks.gvsu.edu/cgi/viewcontent.cgi?article= 1061&context=orpc (accessed 19 September 2020).

[13] See for example https://www.telegraph.co.uk/comment/5166789/ WE-CANT-LET-THE-FAMILY-DIE.html, https://carm.org/ christian-family or https://www.familylife.com/ (accessed 19 September 2020).

[14] For example see https://www.whatchristianswanttoknow.com/ how-does-god-define-family/ (accessed 19 September 2020).

[15] John Bristow, *What Paul Really Said About Women* (New York: HarperCollins, 1991), pp. 35–8.

[16] Gen. 4:1–16.

[17] See for example Mary Pytches, *Who Am I? Discovering Your Identity in Christ* (London: Hodder & Stoughton, 1999), pp. 70–9. There are many excellent books on the way the past presents in the here and now – I particularly recommend *The Presenting Past* by Michael Jacobs (see Bibliography). Psychodynamic counselling is based on examining the relationship between past, present and what happens in the counselling itself.

[18] Others would disagree, and some of the ministries around inner or emotional healing sometimes promise more. It is simply not my experience, professional or personal.

[19] Gen. 45:3.

[20] Mark 3:21; John 7:5.

[21] See for example the place of James in Acts 15 at the Council of Jerusalem, and https://www.escholar.manchester.ac.uk/api/datastream?publicationPid=uk-ac-man-scw:1m2675&datastreamId=POST-PEER-REVIEW-PUBLISHERS.PDFfor a fuller discussion (accessed 19 September 2020).

[22] See Matt. 12:49,50; Jas 2:15; 1 John 3:1; Jas 2:15.

[23] See for example https://www.eauk.org/assets/files/downloads/Reviewing-the-discourse-of-Spiritual-Abuse.pdf, https://www.churchtimes.co.uk/articles/2018/16-february/comment/opinion/understanding-spiritual-abuse or https://www.theguardian.com/uk-news/2019/may/09/church-of-england-put-reputation-above-abuse-victims-needs-inquiry-finds (accessed 19 September 2020).

3 Tears at Goodbyes

[1] Ruth 1:8–10.

[2] Gen. 31:28,55.

[3] Exod. 18:27.

[4] 1 Kgs 19:20.

[5] Luke 9:61,62; Luke 14:33.

[6] Acts 20:37,38.

[7] http://www.yourdailypoem.com/listpoem.jsp?poem_id=2118 (accessed 22 September 2020).

[8] See Kendall, *Finding Our Voice*, p. 152.

[9] Some fear an unhealthy co-dependence, a term which is bandied around. However, in reality that is far more than someone who has insecurities in relation to another person, and outside the scope of this book. See for example https://www.medicalnewstoday.com/articles/319873.php (accessed 21 September 2020).

[10] The other stages are Autonomy vs. shame, Initiative vs. guilt, Industry vs. inferiority, Identity vs. role confusion, Intimacy vs. isolation, Generativity vs. stagnation and Ego integrity vs. despair. See the Bibliography for some of Erikson's books and https://www.simplypsychology.org/Erik-Erikson.html (accessed 19 September 2020).

[11] This phrase is often used in descriptions of transference, the psychological mechanism whereby we respond in one situation as if in another – such as becoming nervous if we need to see a head teacher even as an adult.

4 Tears of Friendship

[1] 1 Sam. 20:41.
[2] 2 Sam. 9:8.
[3] 2 Sam. 4:4.
[4] 1 Sam. 20:13.
[5] The Hobbit trilogy was released in 2012 (*The Hobbit: An Unexpected Journey*), 2013 (*The Hobbit: the Desolation of Smaug*) and 2014 (*The Hobbit: The Battle of the Five Armies*). Distributed by Warner Bros., Metro-Goldwyn-Mayer and New Line Cinema.
[6] Released in three parts in 2001 (*The Fellowship of the Ring*), 2002 (*The Two Towers*) and 2003 (*The Return of the King*). Distributed by New Line Cinema.
[7] 1 Sam. 17.
[8] 1 Sam. 18:1.
[9] 1 Sam. 13:3.
[10] 1 Sam. 14.
[11] 1 Sam. 24.
[12] Not helped by the phenomena of transference, where those being helped experience the other 'as if' they are someone else – including parental transference and erotic transference. In some forms of therapy, such as psychodynamic counselling, this transference can be worked with, but it needs to be handled with great care.
[13] See 1 Sam. 18:3,4.
[14] 1 Samuel 20:17.
[15] As John Goldingay points out, Goldingay, *Walk On: Life, Loss, Trust, and Other Realities*, p. 71.
[16] Deut. 6:5; Matt. 22:37.

[17] David J. Atkinson, et al (ed.), *New Dictionary of Christian Ethics and Pastoral Theology* (Downers Grove, IL: InterVarsity Press, 1995), p. 398.

[18] See 1 Sam. 23:17.

[19] Psalm 54 is prefaced as being written at this time, and a number of psalms relate to David's anguish during this period.

[20] 1 Sam. 23:16.

[21] The exact circumstances are unclear, but it was as a result of the same battle. The most likely explanation is that he killed himself and the Amalekite told a different story assuming that was what David wanted to hear. See 1 Sam. 31 and 2 Sam. 1.

[22] 2 Sam. 1:12.

[23] Mark 8:31–33.

[24] Luke 22:54-62. John 21:15–19 recounts Jesus asking Peter three times 'do you love me' in a gentle healing of the denial.

[25] John 19:25–27.

[26] John 15:15.

5 Tears of Loss

[1] 2 Sam. 12:22,23.

[2] 2 Sam. 18:33.

[3] For example by Colin Murray Parkes, *Bereavement: Studies of Grief in Adult Life* (London: Penguin, 2010) and Elisabeth Kübler-Ross, *On Grief and Grieving: Finding the Meaning of Grief Through the Five Stages of Loss* (London: Simon & Schuster, 2014).

[4] See for example Christopher W. Morgan, *Suffering and the Goodness of God, Theology in Community* (Wheaton, IL: Crossway Books, 2008), or Gerald W. Peterman and Andrew J. Schmutzer, *Between Pain & Grace: A Biblical Theology of Suffering* (Chicago, IL: Moody, 2015).

[5] For example see John E. Colwell, *Why Have You Forsaken Me? A Personal Reflection on the Experience of Desolation* (Milton Keynes: Paternoster, 2009) for a deeply moving application of Ps. 22 to personal difficulty.

[6] See for example William J. Worden, *Grief Counselling and Grief Therapy* (London: Tavistock/Routledge, 1983), pp. 11–17.

[7] Gen. 23:3.

[8] Ruth 1, see also Chapter 3.

[9] Luke 7:11–17.

[10] Luke 24:13–35.

6 Tears of Distress

[1] Job 2:11–13.

[2] This reflects the Jewish custom of sitting shiva. For the first week after the funeral, mourners' physical needs are catered for and they are never left alone, giving them a way to be relieved of duties to begin the journey of grieving.

[3] Job 16:2.

[4] Job 42:3.

[5] Job 38:4.

[6] One example of this self-care is pastoral supervision, the necessity of which for those in the caring professions is being increasingly recognised by denominations and other professional bodies.

[7] Personally, I have found those by Philip Yancey, such as *The Question That Never Goes Away: What is God Up To in a World of Such Tragedy and Pain?* (London: Hodder & Stoughton, 2013) the most helpful.

[8] Notably Ps. 22, which begins with the agonised words of forsakenness which Jesus quotes on the cross.

[9] Jer. 11:18 – 12:6.

[10] See Hab. 1:13.

7 Tears of Fear

[1] Mark 14:32–34.

[2] Aramaic for Thursday. Aramaic was the language spoken by Jesus and the disciples.

3   Among scholars there is some debate whether the Last Supper was a Passover meal or not. I have therefore left it open. The accounts of the Last Supper are Matt. 26:17–30; Mark 14:12–26; Luke 22:7–38 and John 13 – 17 (although it is not clear at which point of the teaching they left). For a good accessible discussion of this point, see Roy Millar, *Come and See* (Watford: Instant Apostle, 2019).

4   John 13:21.

5   For example John B. Watson, Robert Plutchik, and Paul Ekman.

6   There are different opinions on the number of fundamental emotions. See https://www.paulekman.com/universal-emotions/ (accessed 22 September 2020).

7   The topic of animals and emotions still needs further research: it is not clear if animals feel emotions in the same way, but there is certainly evidence of something we might think of as akin to ours.

8   Technically, stress is more a response to pressure, and fear to threat. Clearly, however, there are areas of considerable overlap.

9   Some organisations are listed at the end of this book as a starting place for information in relation to fear and anxiety.

10 Matt. 1:22,23.

11 John 20:19.

12 Prov. 9:10.

13 Prov. 14:27.

14 Ps. 112:1.

15 For example Matt. 1:20 (Joseph), Luke 1:13 (Zechariah), Luke 1:30 (Mary), and Luke 2:10 (the shepherds). See Jostein Gaarder, *The Christmas Mystery* (London: Phoenix House, 1996), p. 12.

16 Ps. 56:3.

17 Rom. 8:38,39.

8 Tears of Gratitude

1   Luke 7:38.

2   Luke 7:44.

3   Luke 7:47.

4   1 Chr. 29:11–13.
5   Luke 17:17,18.
6   See Atkinson, et al (ed.), *New Dictionary of Christian Ethics and Pastoral Theology* (Downers Grove, IL: InterVarsity Press, 1995), p. 881.
7   Ps. 100:4.
8   See for example Eph. 1:5.
9   See Col. 3:15–17.
10   1 Thess. 5:16–18.
11   See for example Acts 18:9–11.
12   See for example Lam. 3:22,23; Matt. 28:20; Eph. 1:16.

9 Tears of Empathy

1   Luke 23:27,44–49.
2   These are not their real names.
3   See Luke 7:11–17; Luke 8:40–56; and John 11.
4   Luke 23:34.
5   The others are congruence and unconditional positive regard.
6   See Luke 8:1–3.
7   Notably the 2004 film *The Passion of the Christ* produced, co-written and directed by Mel Gibson and distributed by Newmarket Films. See also for example https://www1.cbn.com/medical-view-of-the-crucifixion-of-jesus-christ (accessed 19 September 2020).
8   Ps. 22:1; Matt. 27:46; Mark 15:34.
9   We know he is present because Jesus commends his mother into John's care. See John 19:26,27.
10   Millar, *Come and See*, p. 225. Used with permission.
11   © Thomas Keating, 2012 *Invitation to Love: The Way of Christian Contemplation*, Continuum Publishing US, used by permission of Bloomsbury Publishing Inc., p. 150.
12   Groups of people, often disadvantaged, who engage with faith in a way that reads Scripture politically as well as theologically. They are often linked with liberation theology.

13 © Thomas Keating, *Invitation to Love*, Continuum Publishing US, used by permission of Bloomsbury Publishing Inc., p. 150.

10 Tears of Anger

1 John 11:35.
2 © The Jubilate Group. Words from an original text J.S.B. Monsell (1811–75).
3 Ps. 116:15.
4 John 11:25.
5 Luke 7:11–17.
6 Matt. 9:18–26; Mark 5:21–43; Luke 8:40–56.
7 Luke 10:41.
8 John 11:21, *The Message*.
9 John 11:22, *The Message*.
10 John 11:23.
11 See Isa. 65,66.
12 John 11:25,26.
13 John 11:27.
14 John 11:34.
15 I have been impacted, and this section is influenced by, both Tom Wright, *John for Everyone, Part 2, Chapters 11–21* (London: SPCK, 2002), p. 12, and a sermon preached by Phil Hornsey, my then colleague, on the evening of 17 February 2013.
16 John 11:35.
17 Jewish belief at the time was that the spirit remained around the body for three days.
18 John 11:43.
19 See Eph. 4:26, which is an echo of Ps. 4:4.
20 Wright, *John for Everyone, Part 2*, p. 3.
21 See for example Matt. 24:36.
22 John 11:3.
23 Proponents of this teaching include Kenneth Copeland and Kenneth Hagin, among others. For a collection of articles see https://www.christianitytoday.com/ct/topics/p/prosperity-gospel/ (accessed 19 September 2020).

24 This thought was clarified for me by listening to Skip Heitzig teaching on John 11 from an online teaching series from Calvary Church Albuquerque https://www.youtube.com/watch?v=p-4Ials6gKA (accessed 19 September 2020).

25 Such as the story of Jesus driving the money changers from the Temple recounted in Matt. 21:12–17; Mark 11:15–19; Luke 19:45–48; John 2:13–16.

26 John 11:33.

27 See for example Leon Morris, *The Gospel According to John* (London: Marshall, Morgan & Scott, 1971), p. 556 and Merrill C. Tenney, *The Expositor's Bible Commentary: John* (Grand Rapids, MI: Zondervan, 1995), p. 119.

28 1 Corinthians 15:26.

29 For further information on both anger and anxiety, see the NHS website https://www.nhs.uk (accessed 19 September 2020).

30 Jas 1:19.

31 Eph. 4:26.

32 This is widely quoted in numerous sources, including an article in the *New Scientist* which cites it as coming from *The Art of Rhetoric*. See https://www.newscientist.com/article/mg21729032-700-do-get-mad-the-upside-of-anger/ (accessed 19 September 2020).

33 See https://www.bacp.co.uk or https://www.acc-uk.org/ for a list of counsellors in your area.

34 There are a number of children's books on the theme of monsters who turn out to be friendly. These sometimes address common childhood fears such as noises in the dark, but also can be a useful tool in helping children learn that the emotions which they are often afraid of can be befriended. See also Jane Asher and Gerald Scarfe, *Moppy is Angry* (Trowbridge: Positive Press, 2004).

11 Tears of Stress

1 Acts 20:18–19.

2 See Richard Dormandy, *The Madness of St Paul* (Chawton: Redemptorist Publications, 2011), p. 50.

³ Acts 15:36–41.
⁴ 2 Cor. 12:7–9. There are various theories about the nature of this 'thorn', so I have made use of one of them, a difficulty with his eyes.
⁵ This account imagines Luke reflecting, listening to Paul address the elders from Ephesus recounted in Acts 20. It draws on a wider context of Luke's knowledge of Paul. See also 2 Cor. 1:3–11. For the background see Dormandy, *The Madness of St Paul*, pp. 49–57. Barclay says of the time "Something terrible of which the New Testament has no record happened to Paul in Ephesus.' William Barclay, *The Daily Study Bible: The Letters to the Corinthians* (Edinburgh: The Saint Andrew Press, 1975 ed.), p. 154.
⁶ See https://www.simplypsychology.org/SRRS.html (accessed 19 September 2020).
⁷ 2 Cor. 11:24–28.
⁸ See for example Andy Percey, *Infused with Life*, (Milton Keynes: Authentic Media, 2019).
⁹ Ps. 46:10.
¹⁰ Matt. 11:28–30.
¹¹ See https://www.nhs.uk/conditions/cognitive-behavioural-therapy-cbt/ (accessed 19 September 2020).
¹² See for example https://www.cancerresearchuk.org/about-cancer/what-is-cancer/body-systems-and-cancer/the-immune-system-and-cancer#targetText=Cancer%20can%20weaken%20the%20immune%20system%20by%20spreading%20into%20the,making%20so%20many%20blood%20cells (accessed 19 September 2020).

12 Tears Seen by God

¹ Gen. 21:16–18.
² Rom. 8:39.
³ John 11:35.
⁴ Luke 19: 41–44. Jerusalem was besieged and destroyed in AD70 by the Romans after the Jews rebelled against Roman rule.
⁵ Heb. 5:7.

6   Zeph. 3:17.

7   In the Bible account, between chapters 16 and 21 of Genesis Abram and Sarai have name changes to Abraham and Sarah. However, I suspect Hagar would have been unaware either of the change or its significance, and so in her account the names do not change.

8   Gen. 16:2 is usually translated as Sarai building a family through Hagar, but can equally be translated that Sarai will be built up. Ironically, of course, the result is she feels put down.

9   Gen. 16:8.

10 Gen. 16:13.

11 Gen. 21:17.

12 Some of the best speaking and writing about vulnerability in recent years has been by Brené Brown. As a starting place, try listening to her TED talks or look at the books in the bibliography. https://www.ted. com/talks/brene_brown_on_vulnerability?language=en and https:// www.ted.com/talks/brene_brown_listening_to_shame?language=en (both accessed 19 September 2020). See also Claire Musters, *Taking Off the Mask* (Milton Keynes: Authentic Media, 2017).

13 John Goldingay, *After Eating the Apricot* (Carlisle: Paternoster, 1996), p. 95.

14 Such as Dorothy Sölle and Walter Brueggemann. See Goldingay, *After Eating the Apricot*, p. 96.

15 See for example https://www.simplypsychology.org/maslow.html (accessed 19 September 2020).

16 See for example https://www.uktransactionalanalysis.co.uk/ transactional-analysis/key-concepts/strokes (accessed 19 September 2020).

17 See http://www.clairenewton.co.za/my-articles/transactional-analysis-part-ii-the-games-we-play.html#:~:text=A%20stroke%20is%20 a%20unit,one%20person%20recognizes%20another%20 person.&text=Berne%20defined%20this%20requirement%20 of,in%20order%20to%20be%20stroked (accessed 19 September 2020).

18 Luke 1:26–38.

19 Cited in various places including https://www.psychologytoday. com/gb/blog/the-leaders-code/201409/why-you-need-be-seen (accessed 31 October 2019).

20 See Gen. 47.

21 Exod. 2:23,24.
22 Exod. 3:7,8.

13 Unshed Tears

1 Judg. 16:21.
2 Thomas Dixon, *Weeping Britannia: Portrait of a Nation in Tears* (Oxford: Oxford University Press, 2016).
3 Source https://www.phrases.org.uk/meanings/keep-a-stiff-upper-lip.html (accessed 19 September 2020).
4 See for example https://www.researchgate.net/publication/303365863_Gender_and_emotion (accessed 19 September 2020).
5 See https://www.ncbi.nlm.nih.gov/pmc/articles/PMC2610353/ (accessed 19 September 2020).
6 Prov. 22:6.
7 Rom. 12:15, NRSV.
8 Don Francisco, *Beautiful to Me: Collection Vol. II* (Houston: Alliance Music, 1998).
9 See for example Paul Bradbury's *Sowing in Tears: How to Lament in a Church of Praise* (Cambridge: Grove Books, 2007).
10 Matt. 28:20.
11 See Chapter 5, 'Tears of Loss'.

14 Tears and Prayer

1 1 Sam. 1:10.
2 These were the details as recalled by the writer of the piece.
3 1 Sam. 1:2. We don't know if he married Peninnah because Hannah had no children, as it was not unknown for husbands to take additional wives. However, it may well be that Elkanah, clearly a godly man, took a second wife because of Hannah's childlessness. See Nigel A. Jones, *Samuel, the Boy: Life Lessons from*

the First Four Chapters of 1 Samuel (Bloomington, IN: Westbow Press, 2019), pp. 11–12.
4 1 Sam. 1:8.
5 Richard Foster, *Prayer* (London: Hodder & Stoughton, 1992).
6 Ezra 10:1.
7 Foster, *Prayer* (London: Hodder & Stoughton, 1992), pp. 40–46.
8 See Rom. 12:6–8; 1 Cor. 12:8–10,28–30; Eph. 4:11; 1 Pet. 4:11.
9 2 Kgs 20:5.

15 The Ending of Tears

1 Rev. 21:3,4.
2 Jean Gakwandi, with Karin Heidrich, *Solace: The Story of Solace Ministries* (Kigali: Solace Ministries, 2015), p. 28.
3 In Revelation 13:1 a beast emerges from the sea; Revelation 21:1 describes there being no sea.
4 Matt. 1:23.
5 Rev. 21:23; 22:5.
6 As promised in Isa. 25:8; 35:10; 65:19.
7 Matt. 5:4.
8 Rev. 5:4.
9 Rom. 8:22,23.
10 Lev. 26:11,12; Jer. 31:33; Ezek. 37:12; Song 6:3.
11 It had been spoken of in future terms in Rev. 7:17.

Finding Our Voice

*Unsung lives from the Bible
resonating with stories from today*

Jeannie Kendall

The Bible is full of stories of people facing issues that are still
surprisingly relevant today. Within its pages, people have wrestled
with problems such as living with depression, losing a child,
overcoming shame, and searching for meaning. Yet these are not
always the stories of the well-known heroes of faith, but those of
people whose names are not even recorded.

Jeannie Kendall brings these unnamed people to vibrant life.
Their experiences are then mirrored by a relevant testimony from
someone dealing with a similar situation today.

Finding Our Voice masterfully connects the past with the present
day, encouraging us to identify with the characters' stories,
and giving us hope that, whatever the circumstances, we are all
'known to God'.

978-1-78893-037-6

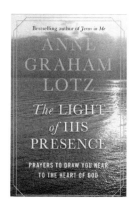

The Light of His Presence

Prayers to draw you near to the heart of God

Anne Graham Lotz

Like many of us, Anne Graham Lotz has struggled with prayer. Over the years, she discovered that writing out her prayers draws her into deeper, more intimate conversations with God.

The Light of His Presence offers forty of these tender, honest prayers for real-life situations as an invitation to deepen your own prayer life through worship, confession, thanksgiving, and intercession. You'll be encouraged to lean more fully into God's promises through this power-packed devotional resource, which includes inspiring quotes from Christians throughout the ages and also has space to journal your own words to God.

As Anne writes, "My prayer for you . . . is that God will use my struggle with prayer to help you overcome yours. And that, as a result, you will be drawn nearer to the heart of God."

978-1-78893-204-2

Slow Down, Show Up & Pray

*Simple shared habits to
renew wellbeing in our local
communities*

Ruth Rice

How can we renew wellbeing in our own lives and in our local
communities?

Looking after our mental health has never been so important.
Many of us want to find simple ways to help our wellbeing that
we can fit into our everyday life.

After suffering her own mental health crisis, Ruth Rice set up the
Renew Wellbeing charity, which helps churches open safe spaces
to help all attend to their mental and emotional health. Packed
full of personal stories, reflective resources and practical guidance,
this book will enable you to maintain your own wellbeing and
encourage churches to provide Renew spaces that help local
communities journey alongside each other to renew wellbeing.

Be present. Be prayerful. Be in partnership.

978-1-78893-183-0

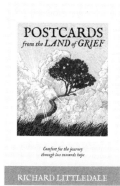

Postcards from the Land of Grief

Comfort for the journey through loss towards hope

Richard Littledale

Losing a loved one can be a lonely, isolating and disorientating experience. Written as postcards from this land of grief, Richard Littledale honestly shares his personal experience in an accessible way that helps fellow travellers to identify their feelings and find hope in the foreign country of bereavement.

Thought-provoking, honest, gentle and ultimately hope-filled, this is a helpful companion for anyone dealing with loss.

978-1-78893-071-0

A Beautiful Tapestry

*Two ordinary women,
one amazing God,
many lives transformed*

*Tracy Williamson
with Marilyn Baker*

Being blind, Marilyn's childhood was one of increasing isolation whilst Tracy's was marked by deafness and low self-esteem. Yet from these most unlikely of origins, God brought these two remarkable ladies together in the most hilarious fashion and gave them a joint vision to work together through Marilyn Baker Ministries.

Through their work in prisons, concerts, retreats, conferences and prayer ministry, they have seen many lives transformed by the power of God's love. Many of those testimonies are included in this book, showing that God is indeed weaving a beautiful tapestry in all our lives. Each individual strand of yarn isn't much in itself, but when woven together an amazing picture emerges as he uses us in our weakness to show the beauty of his love to others.

978-1-78893-156-4

Infused with Life

*Exploring God's gift of rest in
a world of busyness*

Andy Percey

In a stressful, task-orientated life, we know the importance of rest,
but it is too often pushed out of our busy schedules.

Join Andy Percey as he reveals that rest is actually God's good gift to
us, provided for us to experience a balance in our lives that isn't just
about rest as recovery, but rest as harmony with our Creator and the
world he has made.

By learning to practise life-giving rhythms of rest, we can be infused
with the very best of the life God freely gives us.

978-1-78893-065-9

Authentic

We trust you enjoyed reading this book from Authentic. If you want to be informed of any new titles from this author and other releases you can sign up to the Authentic newsletter by scanning below:

Online:
authenticmedia.co.uk

Follow us: